W9-BIG-878

Phonics in Proper Perspective

NINTH EDITION

Arthur W. Heilman
Professor Emeritus
Pennsylvania State University

With thanks to **Theresa Reagan-Donk** *of Western Michigan University*
for her contributions to this edition

Merrill
Prentice Hall

Upper Saddle River, New Jersey
Columbus, Ohio

Library of Congress Cataloging-in-Publication Data
Heilman, Arthur W.
    Phonics in proper perspective / Arthur W. Heilman — 9th ed.
        p. cm.
    Includes bibliographical references and index.
    ISBN 0-13-034345-5
    1. Reading—Phonetic method.   I. Title
LB1573.3. H44 2002
372.46'5—dc21

00-066822

Vice President and Publisher: Jeffery W. Johnston
Editor: Linda Ashe Montgomery
Editorial Assistant: Lori Jones
Production Editor: Linda Hillis Bayma
Project Coordination and Text Design: Carlisle Publishers Services
Design Coordinator: Diane C. Lorenzo
Cover Design: Jason Moore
Cover Art: SuperStock
Production Manager: Pamela D. Bennett
Director of Marketing: Kevin Flanagan
Marketing Manager: Krista Groshong
Marketing Coordinator: Barbara Koontz

This book was set in Frutiger Light by Carlisle Communications, Ltd., and was printed and bound by R.R. Donnelley & Sons Company. The cover was printed by The Lehigh Press, Inc.

Prentice-Hall International (UK) Limited, *London*
Prentice-Hall of Australia Pty. Limited, *Sydney*
Prentice-Hall Canada, Inc., *Toronto*
Prentice-Hall Hispanoamericana, S.A., *Mexico*
Prentice-Hall of India Private Limited, *New Delhi*
Prentice-Hall of Japan, Inc., *Tokyo*
Prentice-Hall Singapore Pte. Ltd.
Editora Prentice-Hall do Brasil, Ltda., *Rio de Janeiro*

10 9 8 7 6 5 4 3 2
ISBN 0-13-034345-5

Preface

The purpose of this book is to provide both the experienced and the prospective teacher with materials that will lead to better understanding of the following:

- The purpose and limitations of phonics instruction as it relates to teaching reading
- Concrete practices to follow in teaching the various steps in phonics analysis
- The rationale that underlies particular instructional practices

The material in this book reflects several premises:

- Phonics is an important part of teaching beginning reading.
- Teachers should be knowledgeable about the purpose of phonics instruction and its limitations.
- For children to make normal progress in learning to read, they must learn to associate printed letter forms with the speech sounds they represent.
- Beginning reading instruction must not mislead children into thinking that reading is sounding out letters, or learning sight words, or using context clues.

Learning to read involves *all* these skills in the right combination. The optimum amount of phonics instruction for each child is the absolute minimum the child needs to become an independent reader. Excessive phonics instruction will usurp time that should be devoted to reading, can destroy children's interest in reading, and may lead critics to attack phonics instruction rather than bad phonics instruction.

For the ninth edition, I would like to thank the following reviewers who provided valuable comments and suggestions: Martha Cocchiarella, Arizona State University; Wanda Hedrick, The University of Texas at San Antonio; Rosie Webb Joels, The University of Central Florida; Stephanie Steffey, San Jose State University; Karen R. Travis, Southwestern Oklahoma State University; and Bonita F. Williams, Columbus State University.

Contents

Chapter 1

PHONICS: PURPOSE AND LIMITATIONS

*T*he purpose of phonics instruction is to teach beginning readers that printed letters and letter combinations represent speech sounds heard in words. In applying phonic skills to an unknown word, the reader blends a series of sounds dictated by the order in which particular letters occur in the printed word. One needs this ability to arrive at the pronunciation of printed word symbols that are not instantly recognized. Obviously, if one recognizes a printed word, he should not puzzle over the speech sounds represented by the individual letters.

"Arriving at the pronunciation" of a word does not mean learning *how* to pronounce that word. In most reading situations, particularly in the primary grades, the readers know the pronunciation of practically all words they will meet in their reading. What they do not know is that the printed word symbol *represents* the pronunciation of a particular word they use and understand in oral language. Through phonic analysis they resolve this dilemma.

THE STUDY OF PHONICS

Phonics is not a *method* of teaching reading, nor is it the same as phonetics. Phonics is one of a number of ways a child may "solve" words not known as sight words. Phonics instruction is concerned with teaching letter-sound relationships *only as they relate to learning to read.* English spelling patterns being what they are, children will sometimes arrive at only a close approximation of the needed sounds. They may pronounce *broad* so it rhymes with *road,* or *fath* (in father) so that it rhymes with *path.* Fortunately, if they are reading for meaning, they will instantly correct these errors. After a few such self-corrections, they will never again make these particular mistakes.

Phonetics is much more precise. It is the scientific study of the sound systems of language. Phoneticians are scientists. They know much more about speech sounds and spelling patterns than is necessary for children to know while learning to read, or for teachers to teach when the goal is teaching reading.

Linguists rightfully urge reading teachers not to confuse phonics with phonetics. Phonetics is a science; the teaching of reading is not. While it is true that phonics is based on phonetics, linguists should not be distressed when they observe a phonics instruction program that does not include certain known phonetic data. First and second graders do not need to be exposed to all the phonetic data that have been assembled. Learning to read is a complicated process, and it need not be complicated further simply because a vast body of phonetic data exists. In teaching reading, one must hold to the scientific principle that instruction must follow the most economical path to its chosen goal. A guideline for instruction is that *the optimum amount of phonics instruction a child should be exposed to is the minimum the child needs to become an independent reader.* This is certainly not the way to become a linguist, but it is good pedagogy for beginning reading instruction.

Terminology

In recent years, noticeable confusion has accompanied discussions of reading because the meaning of some of the terms used has been vague or misleading. To eliminate further confusion, we will briefly define a few basic terms.

Alphabetic principle. Graphic symbols have been devised for representing a large number of spoken languages. Three types of writing (picture, ideographic, and alphabetic) represent the English words or concepts *car, carp,* and *carpet* in Figure 1–1.

The picture and ideographic writing are purely arbitrary. The ideographs are not taken from an established language. The most important feature of the ideographic

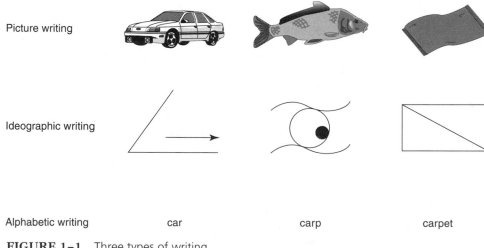

Picture writing

Ideographic writing

Alphabetic writing   car   carp   carpet

FIGURE 1–1   Three types of writing

writing is that there are no common features in the three symbols. The alphabetic writing is also arbitrary, but it is based on the alphabetic principle: the letter symbols and their order of occurrence have been universally agreed upon since they are taken from English writing. The first three letter symbols in each word are identical. They signal the reader to blend the same three speech sounds (phonemes) if the goal is to arrive at the spoken word that the various letter configurations represent. In the case of *carp* and *carpet*, the reader must blend still other phonemes.

There are many other spoken words in which one hears the same three phonemes in the same sequence. The graphic representation of these speech sounds will be the same in a number of printed words: *carnival, cardinal, card, cartoon*. In English writing, however, one may see the graphic symbols *car* and find that they represent different phonemes from the ones under discussion (*carol, care, career, caress, caret*).

Digraph. A digraph is a combination of two letters that represent one speech sound (consonant examples: *ch*urch, *sh*ow, *th*ank; vowel examples: b*ee*t, c*oa*t, m*ai*l).

Diphthong. A diphthong is a vowel blend: two adjacent vowels, each of which is sounded (ou in h*ou*se, oi in *oi*l, oy in b*oy*, ow in h*ow*).

Grapheme. A grapheme is a written or printed letter symbol used to represent a speech sound or phoneme.

Grapheme-phoneme relationship. This term refers to the relationship between printed letters and the sounds they represent; it also covers the deviations found in such a relationship. Thus, while English writing is based on an alphabetic code, there is not a one-to-one relationship between graphemes (printed symbols) and the phonemes (speech sounds) they represent. Some printed symbols represent several different sounds (car, caress, cake), and one speech sound may be represented by many different letters or combinations of letters (which we will discuss later in this chapter). To a great extent, this problem stems from the spelling patterns of words that have become established in English writing.

Morphemes. These are the smallest meaningful units of language. The word *cat* is a morpheme whose pronunciation consists of three phonemes. If one wishes to speak of more than one cat, the letter *s* forming the plural *cats* becomes a morpheme, since it changes the meaning (as does the possessive *'s* in the *cat's* dinner).

There are two classes of morphemes, free and bound. The former functions independently in any utterance (*house, lock, man, want*). Bound morphemes consist of prefixes, suffixes, and inflectional endings and must combine with other morphemes (house*s*, *un*lock, man*'s*, want*ed*).

Onset. An initial consonant or consonant cluster is an onset. In the word *name*, *n* is the onset; in the word *blame*, *bl* is the onset.

Phoneme. A phoneme is the smallest unit of sound in a language that distinguishes one word from another. Pronouncing the word *cat* involves blending three phonemes: /k/ /æ/ /t/.

Phonemic awareness. This term refers to the knowledge or understanding that speech consists of a series of sounds and that individual words can be divided into phonemes.

Phonemic segmentation. Breaking a syllable or word into its constituent phonemes [top = /t/ /o/ /p/].

Phonetic method. This is a vague term that once was used to indicate instruction that included phonics, emphasized phonics, or overemphasized phonics. Eventually it acquired the polar connotation of "pro-phonics" and "anti-sight-word method." (We will discuss this dichotomy in Chapter 2.)

Phonetics. This term refers to the segment of linguistic science that deals with (a) speech sounds; (b) how these sounds are made vocally; (c) sound changes that develop in languages; and (d) the relation of speech sounds to the total language process. All phonics instruction is derived from phonetics, but phonics as it relates to reading utilizes only a relatively small portion of the body of knowledge identified as phonetics.

Phonic analysis. This is the process of applying knowledge of letter-sound relationships, that is, blending the sounds represented by letters so as to arrive at the pronunciation of printed words.

Phonics instruction. Phonics instruction is a facet of reading instruction that (a) leads the child to understand that printed letters in printed words represent the speech sounds heard when words are pronounced; and (b) involves the actual teaching of which sound is associated with a particular letter or combination of letters.

Rime. A rime is the vowel or vowel and consonant(s) that follow the onset. In the word *name, ame* is the rime.

Schwa. The schwa sound is a diminished stress, or a softening of the vowel sound. Schwa is represented by the symbol ə (bedlam = bed ləm; beckon = bek' ən). Any of the vowels may represent the schwa sound.

Sight vocabulary. A sight vocabulary includes any words a reader recognizes instantly, without having to resort to any word-recognition strategies.

Sight-word method. The term *sight-word method* is an abstraction rather than a description of reading instruction. Some beginning reading materials developed prior to the mid nineteen fifties, however, advocated teaching a limited number of sight words before phonic analysis was introduced. The term *sight-word method* became common even though it actually described only this initial teaching procedure. Gradually the term was used to imply the existence of an instructional approach that allegedly proscribed phonics and advocated teaching every new word by sight only.

Word analysis.   This is an inclusive term that refers to all methods of word recognition. Phonics is one such method.

Limitations of Phonics

Phonics instruction does have limitations. Knowing this fact helps us avoid expecting too much of our lessons. It also helps us see why children need other related word recognition skills.

VARIABILITY OF LETTER-SOUNDS IN ENGLISH

The greatest limitation of the use of phonics is the spelling patterns of many English words. Although written English is alphabetic, the irregular spellings of words prevent anything like a one-to-one relationship between letters seen and sounds heard. Some of the reasons for, and examples of, this problem include the following.

1. Many English words have come from other languages such as Latin, Greek, French, and German (*waive, alias, corps, debris, alien, buoy, feint, bouquet*). The spelling of these words is often confusing.
2. A given letter, or letters, may represent different sounds in different words: c*ow* = ow, l*ow* = ō; c*an* = ă, c*ane* = ā, *c*ap = k, *c*ity = s; bu*s* = s, hi*s* = z, mea*s*ure = zh.
3. The following illustrate some of the variability found in English words. Some words (homonyms) are (a) pronounced the same, (b) spelled differently, and (c) each is phonetically "lawful."

weak—week	meat—meet	heal—heel	beat—beet
peal—peel	real—reel	peak—peek	steal—steel

In these examples, the generalization that applies to both spellings is *when there are two adjacent vowels in a word, usually the first is long and the second is not sounded.*
   One word in each of the following pairs is governed by this phonic generalization; the other is not.

vain	rain	peace	wait
vein	reign	piece	weight

4. In hundreds of English words, a letter or letters may represent no sound.

    nigh̷t   comḃ   of̷ten   w̷rong

5. A word may have one or more letters not sounded that differentiate it from another word pronounced exactly the same.

new	our	plum	cent	no
knew	hour	plumb	scent	know

6. The long sound of vowels may be represented by any of these and other combinations in words.

	day	they	fate	sail	reign	great
ā =	ay	ey	a(e)	ai	ei	ea
	feet	meat	deceive	brief	ski	key
ē =	ee	ea	ei	ie	i	ey
	my	kite	pie	height	buy	guide
ī =	y	i(e)	ie	ei	uy	ui
	show	hold	boat	note	go	sew
ō =	ow	o(+ ld)	oa	o(e)	o	ew
	flew	view	tube	due	suit	you
ū =	ew	iew	u	ue	ui	ou

One of the problems in teaching letter-sound relationships is that dozens of "rules" or "generalizations" have been developed to help learners arrive at the pronunciation of words they do not recognize. The following discussion focuses on three of the most widely used generalizations and their limited efficacy resulting from numerous exceptions.

1. *When two vowels are side by side in a word, the first usually has its long sound and the second is not sounded.*

    Rule applies: boat, rain, meat, week, soap, sail, need
    Exceptions: been, said, chief, dead, field, head, their

2. *When a word has two vowels, the second being final e, the first usually has its long sound and the final e is not sounded.*

    Rule applies: ride, pale, hate, bite, dime, hide, cane, cute
    Exceptions: love, done, have, come, give, none, once

3. *A single vowel in medial position in a word or syllable usually has its short sound.*

Extensive research has shown that the first two rules apply less than fifty percent of the time in high-frequency words. The third generalization can be useful to children learning to read. It applies to enough high-frequency words to justify calling it to students' attention. However, there is no phonetic rule that will apply to all words that meet the criteria the rule sets forth. The following illustrates how, when a rule does not apply to a number of words, a new rule emerges to cover this situation.

Exception A: *hold, cold, bold, gold; bolt, colt*
New rule: The single vowel *o,* followed by *ld* or *lt,* has its long sound.

Exception B: *car, fir, fur, her, for, part, bird, hurt, perch, corn*
New rule: A vowel followed by *r* has neither its long nor short sound—the vowel sound is modified by the *r.*

Exception C: *wild, mild, child; find, kind, mind, blind*
New rule: The vowel *i* before *ld* or *nd* is usually long.

Exception D: *fall, call, ball; salt, malt, halt*
New rule: The vowel *a* followed by *ll* or *lt* is pronounced like *aw* (ball = bawl).

Exception E: *high, sigh; light, night, bright, flight*
New rule: The vowel *i* in *igh* and *ight* words is usually long.

Other exceptions: s*i*gn = (i); w*a*s = (u); b*o*th = (ō); fr*o*nt = (u)

These examples deal only with monosyllabic words containing a single vowel in a medial position. There are also a number of consonant irregularities, discussed in Chapter 5, but none of these represent the large number of sounding options that are characteristic of vowels. The exceptions to the basic rule are only the major ones that might logically be dealt with in teaching reading, and the words listed represent only a small fraction of those that could be cited. As rules become more involved and cover fewer and fewer actual words, one might question the relationship between learning these rules and learning the process called reading.

For many years, teachers have had considerable data available that focus on the frequency with which various phonic rules apply to words children will meet in their primary and elementary school experiences. Studies by Oaks (1952), Clymer (1962), Bailey (1967), Emans (1967), Burmeister (1968), and Burrows and Lourie (1963) are in agreement in their findings that there are a significant number of exceptions to generalizations covering vowel sounds.

The educational issue is not arriving at a universally agreed upon list of rules to be taught. The real problem, which is much more complicated, is what happens to learners under various types of instruction that focus on rules. What types of attack strategies do children develop? There is little information to guide teachers. Those who have worked extensively with impaired readers have undoubtedly encountered some children who are rule oriented. Some of these children persist in trying to make the rule fit even when the word they are attacking is an exception. Others can cite the rule and still are unable to apply it to words that it covers.

Despite the absence of data that might serve as a guide for teaching phonic generalizations, teachers must decide on the teaching strategies they will use. They may choose instructional materials that make a fetish of memorizing phonic generalizations.

They might, on the other hand, present a series of words governed by a particular rule and invite children to formulate a generalization. The latter course seems preferable, not just because it fits under the rubric *discovery method,* but because it permits children to work with concepts they can understand. Furthermore, it relieves the learning situation of a certain degree of rigidity and reduces the finality that is usually associated with a rule.

Chapter 2

PHONICS: HISTORY AND CONTROVERSY

America is in the latter stages of repealing the dream of universal free education and the goal of educating all children to the maximum of their ability. Neither educators nor their critics believe the schools can educate all of the children that our society delivers to the schools. For decades, criticism of American education has focused on reading, or more precisely, on the phonics component of that instruction.

Should educators, and specifically reading teachers, be conversant with past instructional methods and materials? It might be difficult to establish that knowledge of this history is essential for successful teaching of reading. However, such knowledge can be helpful in understanding some of the problems, attitudes, and misunderstandings that have been and still are associated with American reading instruction. The instructional programs and philosophies presented in the following discussion—both for and against phonics—were all devised by adults, allegedly with the best interests of children in mind. However, hindsight suggests the danger of permitting the beliefs of single-minded crusaders to go unchallenged.

EARLY TRENDS

During the latter part of the nineteenth century, beginning reading instruction stressed the teaching of the ABCs. Children were taught to recite the names of the letters that made up unknown words met in reading. It was believed that letter naming would provide the necessary phonetic clues for arriving at the spoken word the printed symbols represented. In essence, this was a spelling approach, since letter names often have little resemblance to speech sounds represented by letters (*come* = *see oh em ee* = *kum*). This approach, abandoned because it didn't work, was revived in 1961 by Leonard Bloomfield.

Prior to 1900, and continuing for over a decade, emphasis shifted from drill on letter names to drill on the sounds of the various letters. Rebecca Pollard's *Synthetic Method,* introduced in 1889, advocated reducing reading to a number of mechanical procedures, each of which focused on a unit smaller than a word. Reading became very mechanistic and, when mastered, often produced individuals who were adept at working their way through a given word. The result among both teachers and pupils was that reading became equated with "facility in calling words." A few of the recommended procedures of this method include the following.

1. Drills in articulation were to precede any attempt at reading. The child was to drill on the "sounds of letters." Then the child would be able, it was reasoned, to attack whole words.
2. Single consonants were "sounded." Each consonant was given a sound equivalent to a syllable. Thus, *b, c, d, p, h,* and *t* were sounded *buh, cuh, duh, puh, huh,* and *tuh.*
3. Drills on word families were stressed without regard for word meanings. Sometimes children memorized lists of words ending in such common family phonograms as *ill, am, ick, ate, old,* and *ack.*
4. Diacritical markings were introduced in first grade, and children drilled on "marking sentences." For example: The ghŏst wăs a cŏmmŏn sīght near the wrĕck. He knew the īsland was ĕmpty.

This and similar approaches had a number of weaknesses, including the following.

1. The sounds assigned to consonant letters were arbitrary.
2. Letter sounds were overemphasized and taught in isolation (*buh-ah-tuh* = *bat*).
3. This was true also as drill on vowel letter sounds was combined with initial consonant sounds (*ba, da, ha, ma, pa, ra*).
4. Drill instruction was not related to actual words or to actual reading.

It is easy to see that this type of instruction placed little emphasis on reading as a meaning-making process. As children performed these ritualistic drills, they developed an inappropriate concept of reading that negatively influenced their reading behavior.

While these so-called phonics instructional practices were indefensible, the response to these excesses was equally unrealistic. The revolt against the say-the-letters-ignore-the-meaning era resulted in behavior that seemed to suggest that children might learn to read if *words* were bypassed and instruction began immediately with larger units of print. These were called "meaning-bearing units," and it was suggested that beginning instruction focus on sentences, stories, and real literature.

In the book *American Reading Instruction (1934),* Nila B. Smith describes this period. Her book is the source for the several publications cited in the following brief discussion.

In 1895, George L. Farham published *The Sentence Method of Teaching Reading* (cited in Smith, 1934, p. 140). This approach advocated using whole sentences or even stories as a starting point. The teacher would read these "whole messages" to the class and repeat them many times. The children would then recite the material several times. The goal was to have children learn these passages. If they were successful, these activities were somehow equated with reading. Children were not taught to identify any of the words, except perhaps by their visual patterns. Thus, nothing they learned could transfer to the next reading experience if other words were involved. This approach became more aptly named when Charles McMurray, in 1897, published *The Method of Recitation* (cited in Smith, 1934, p. 117).

When support for the sentence-and-story-recitation methods waned, there emerged a movement to use literature as the reading curriculum. A number of reading textbooks published in this era are cited by Smith (1934, p. 122):

Stepping Stones to Literature (1897)

Graded Literature Series (1899)

Special Methods in Reading of Complete English Classics (1899)

In the latter text it was suggested that materials such as *Snow Bound, The Great Stone Face,* and *Julius Caesar* be read and studied as complete works. In agreement, Charles W. Eliot, then president of Harvard University, suggested that existing reading textbooks be removed because they were not *real* literature, just excerpts from literature. Smith (1934) wrote, "We found that between the approximate dates of 1880 and 1918 educators considered the supreme function of reading instruction to be that of developing appreciation for and permanent interest in literature" (p. 185).

The era of literature emphasis just sketched had an elitist component. This reading curriculum might possibly have made sense for that minority of young people destined for more advanced education, college, and the professions. The socioeconomic status of this group was a guarantee that they would acquire (in or out of school) the prerequisite of actually knowing how to read. The problem was that the majority of children in the public schools were not learning reading skills adequate to follow the literature curriculum.

REALITY CHECK: BASAL PROGRAMS

There were a number of changes taking place in American society that raised serious questions about the utility of literature as the reading curriculum. Compulsory education laws kept children in school longer, and students' inability to read caused the schools problems. Also, the workplace was demanding a higher level of literacy. Thus, the inability to read was noticed and became an issue in both the school and the larger community.

The result was a challenge to the magnificent obsession that exposure to literature (sans reading ability) could result in students reading literature. The alternative was to be to teach children to read—then teach the literature. Instruction would have to change. It would be slower, more obvious, more direct. Actual teaching materials could not continue to be adult-critiqued literature. To borrow a future criticism, there had to be a "dumbing down" of the reading curriculum.

This was accomplished with the emergence of a new wave of basal reading materials. Graded materials for primary-level instruction (grades 1–6) had been available for more than a century. However, these new materials were definitely a break with tradition. The chief difference was the dual thrust of reading textbooks accompanied by increased emphasis on workbooks that emphasized, taught, and reviewed reading skills. Several characteristics of these materials should be noted.

1. The difficulty level of the reading materials was held to an absolute minimum by severely controlling and limiting the introduction of printed words. After

months of instruction, children were still dealing with stories limited to a vocabulary of 60 to 80 words.

2. This very limited vocabulary necessitated interminable repetition of words in the text materials. This was deadly for students, teachers, parents, and society. Nevertheless, the basals remained the materials of choice for several decades.

3. Basal programs were able to temporarily avoid entanglement in the polar positions regarding teaching phonics. There is no evidence of a deliberate effort to foster the appearance of neutrality in regard to phonics instruction. However, the actual reading textbooks contained little or no overt teaching of letter-sound relationships, while the workbook segments of the programs taught and reviewed phonics skills at every level. Thus, whatever position one preferred in regard to teaching phonics could be accommodated by how one chose to use and emphasize various parts of these programs.

Teachers were poorly served by this laissez-faire attitude toward phonics. There was little guidance in regard to the introduction, emphasis, or methodology involved in teaching phonics. For some teachers, this instruction became less deliberate and less systematic. Many children experienced difficulty in becoming independent readers. In other classrooms, the workbooks became a substitute for teaching. There, mindless repetition of seatwork posing as reading turned children away from reading.

Teacher indecision about instructional practices left fertile ground for the reemergence of an old idea. During the 1850s and later, the conventional wisdom had been that beginning reading instruction should focus on children learning to recognize whole words. This practice could lead to success for a limited time. Children could learn to differentiate among a number of words relying on visual cues only. However, progress in learning broke down when children started to meet an avalanche of unknown words that were very similar in their visual patterns. The word method then gave way to the sentence method and the literature emphasis mentioned previously. The ambivalent attitude toward phonics instruction opened the door to a new version of the whole-word approach.

SIGHT-WORD METHOD VERSUS PHONETIC METHOD

Gradually, the conventional wisdom decreed that children should learn a number of sight words prior to receiving any phonics instruction. This philosophy, then reflected in many of the basal materials that were used in the schools, had a tendency to delay phonics instruction. Somehow this instructional philosophy became labeled the "sight-word method."

It is probably safe to surmise that the term *sight-word method* led some people to believe that there was such a method. Since the term omits any reference to phonics, some people might have inferred that phonics was meant to be excluded. At the other end of the continuum, the same type of illogical labeling was taking place. A belief that letter-sound relationships should be taught made one an advocate of the *phonetic method*. Gradually, these two terms took on an either-or connotation, and these were the only positions available. One was either pro-phonics and opposed to teaching sight words or vice versa.

Although these labels could not, and did not, describe any instructional programs in the schools, they completely dominated the debate on reading instruction. Hundreds of research articles, most of them of dubious quality, divided quite evenly on espousing either the phonetic or sight-word method. Thus, the 20-year period preceding the 1950s did not witness any significant modifications in either instructional materials or methodology. All of the widely used basal reading programs were quite similar.

During this period, some children learned to read, some were definitely impaired readers, and very few loved to read. At reading conferences and conventions, teachers constantly asked, "How do you motivate children to read?" This question persisted because it never received a serious answer. There was no responsible answer as long as the then-existing reading curriculum was in place. Children were being asked to read bland, unchildlike materials while instruction moved them much too slowly toward becoming independent readers. Few suspected that things were about to get worse.

CRITICISM LEADS TO NEW PHONICS MATERIALS

As criticism of children's reading ability increased, hostility to existing instructional materials mounted. During the 1950s, there were more focus and debate on reading instruction and more calls for change than there had been in any previous period. The major catalyst for change was a book written with the fervor that only a true believer could muster: in 1955, Rudolph Flesch published the book *Why Johnny Can't Read*.

Flesch's book came on the scene at exactly the right time. It was simplistic, but written with enough unabashed authority that it was hailed as a panacea. *Why Johnny Can't Read* was one dimensional in that lack of phonics instruction was the alleged problem, and more phonics was the only acceptable solution. There was, Flesch claimed, a conspiracy within the reading establishment to prevent the teaching of phonics. Institutions involved with teacher preparation were a part of, and a moving force behind, this conspiracy. Having identified the problem, Flesch advanced a solution: Teach phonics my way and there will be no failures in learning to read. This publication eventually triggered a strong swing of the pendulum back to phonics instruction.

While Flesch was instrumental in arousing interest in phonics, his suggestions relative to teaching were quite primitive. His material consisted mostly of lists of words presenting different letter-sound patterns. Drill on these word lists was the extent of his instructional program. It was impossible for teachers to use these lists as a basis for instruction.

However, this instructional vacuum was soon filled with a number of new methods and materials that were developed and vigorously promoted. A number of supplementary "phonics emphasis" materials such as flash cards, workbooks, and tape recordings were offered as add-ons for any existing programs. In addition, whole new instructional programs with their own teaching materials were developed, including *Programmed Reading* (n.d.), *Words in Color* (1962), and the *Initial Teaching Alphabet* (ITA) (1963).

This new emphasis on code-cracking (phonics instruction) also spawned a set of instructional materials that were alleged to focus on cracking the code. However, their main thrust was total opposition to teaching any real phonics or letter-sound relationships. To illustrate the scope, philosophy, and inherent weaknesses of these new programs, two will be briefly summarized here. These are the *ITA,* which represented a strong phonics emphasis, and the *Linguistic Regular Spelling* program, which proscribed the teaching of phonics.

THE INITIAL TEACHING ALPHABET (ITA)

The Initial Teaching Alphabet was developed in England by Sir James Pitman in order to achieve a more uniform letter-seen–sound-heard relationship in English writing. This was first called the Augmented Roman Alphabet, since it consisted of 44 rather than 26 letter symbols (Figure 2–1).

FIGURE 2–1   Pitman's Initial Teaching Alphabet (ITA)

Source: From Richard Fink and Patricia Keiserman, ITA Teacher Training Workbook and Guide (New York: Initial Teaching Alphabet Publications, 1969). Reprinted by permission.

The use of 44 symbols permits a much closer approximation of a one-to-one relationship between printed letters and the sounds they represent. Obviously, teaching with the ITA involved the development and use of reading materials printed in the ITA. Since the materials were concerned only with initial instruction, learners had to transfer from the ITA materials to materials printed in regular orthography sometime near the end of first grade.

The ITA Instructional Program

The ITA involved more than just the use of a modified orthography. Several salient instructional features were an integral part of its methodology.

1. Children were not taught letter names, but they were taught that each ITA symbol represented a particular sound. Early instruction consisted of systematic teaching of these symbol-sound relationships.
2. From the very beginning of instruction, children were taught to write using the ITA symbols. Writing, which involves spelling of words, reinforced the phonics instruction (letter-sound relationships).
3. In ITA instruction, children learned only the lowercase letters. Capitals were indicated simply by making the letter larger. Thus, the child did not have to deal with two different symbols for the same letter (Aa, Bb, Cc, Dd, Ee, Ff, Gg, Hh) in the initial stages of learning to read and write. In essence, what this practice did was to delay for a time the child's need to master both sets of symbols.
4. Promotional materials for the ITA claimed that there was a high degree of compatibility between ITA and traditional spellings. A fact ignored was that ITA materials frequently resorted to phonetic respelling of irregularly spelled words.

ITA: Postponing the Difficult

As the title *Initial Teaching Alphabet* implies, this was an approach that focused on beginning reading only. Beginning reading tasks were simplified in several ways.

1. Capital letter forms were not introduced.
2. Irregularly spelled words were respelled.
3. All long vowel sounds were represented by two adjacent vowel letters.

Particular attention had to be paid to the various respellings, which resulted in a high degree of consistency between letters seen and sounds heard. This would have had great virtue if it had represented a real spelling reform. However, at the time of transfer, children had to face the reality of irregular spellings while having been taught that words could be sounded by blending the sounds of the letters seen. This mind set that was developed during initial teaching could easily inhibit growth when irregular spellings were met in great profusion in traditional orthography. Table 2–1 illustrates respellings that have nothing to do with the modified alphabet.

Some of these respellings change the visual pattern of words quite drastically, which does not facilitate transfer to traditional print and spelling. While this practice might have resulted in a rapid start in beginning reading, it had minimal effects on

---

TABLE 2-1 *Initial Teaching Alphabet Respellings*

enough – – – – – – enuf	anyone – – – – – – enywun	said – – – – – – – sed
once – – – – – – – – wuns	large – – – – – – – larj	next – – – – – – – nekst
lovely – – – – – – – – luvly	many – – – – – – – meny	George – – – – – Jorj
crossed – – – – – – crosst	some – – – – – – – sum	one – – – – – – – wun
six – – – – – – – – – siks	money – – – – – – muny	couple – – – – – – cupl
glove – – – – – – – – gluv	laugh – – – – – – – laf	none – – – – – – – nun
wax – – – – – – – – waks	ought – – – – – – – aut	someone – – – – sumwun
yacht – – – – – – – – yot	tough – – – – – – – tuf	trouble – – – – – –trubl

---

TABLE 2-2 *Initial Teaching Alphabet Two-Vowel Generation*

also – – – – – – – – – auls œ	night – – – – – – – niet	find – – – – – – – f iend
their – – – – – – – – thær	so – – – – – – – – – s œ	seized – – – – – – s ee zd
there – – – – – – – thær	idea – – – – – – – – ie d ee a	wife – – – – – – – w ie f
I – – – – – – – – – – ie	most – – – – – – – mœst	walked – – – – – w au kt
knows – – – – – – n œs	came – – – – – – – c æm	ate – – – – – – – æt
fire – – – – – – – – fie r	lace – – – – – – – – l æ s	owe – – – – – – – œ
my – – – – – – – – – m ie	phone – – – – – f œ n	page – – – – – – pæj
sight – – – – – – – sie t	weigh – – – – – – w æ	gave – – – – – – – g æ v
giant – – – – – – – j ie ant	nice – – – – – – – – n ie s	people – – – – – p ee pl
eyes – – – – – – – ie s	five – – – – – – – f ie v	life – – – – – – – l ie f

---

children cracking the main code. They eventually had to deal with irregular words when they transferred to traditional orthography.

In addition to the phonetic respellings, which did not involve any of the new ITA characters, many spelling changes involved a reshuffling of vowels. The vowel changes and transpositions were made so that the spelling would follow the "two-vowel generalization": when two vowels come together, the first has its long sound and the second is silent. Some examples of this are presented in Table 2–2.

Transfer from the ITA to Traditional Orthography

Concurrently with the introduction and use of the ITA in America, there were assurances from many quarters that transfer from the ITA to traditional print would not pose a problem. This optimism was allegedly grounded on reports from England. While John Downing of England was actively promoting the experimental use of the ITA in America, his 1963 publication, *Experiments with Pitman's Initial Teaching Alphabet in British Schools,* contained a note of caution on the issue of transfer:

> If teachers *opinions* are supported by the results of the objective tests conducted last month [March 1963], we may feel encouraged in *our hopes* that all children will pass through the transfer stage with success, but *we must urge the greatest caution in drawing final conclusions or taking action on the basis of this preliminary trial.* (p. 125)

Downing's caution was vindicated by the outcome of studies in England and America. In the December 1967 issue of *Elementary English,* Downing stated,

> Although teachers' subjective impressions of the transition stage have suggested that it is smooth and effortless, test results show that i.t.a. students from about mid-second year until about mid-third year do not read t.o. [traditional orthography] as well as they read i.t.a. a few weeks or even months previously. . . . More specifically, the British experiments show that children are not transferring from i.t.a. to t.o. in quite the way originally predicted. (p. 849)

Reading achievement resulting from the use of the ITA failed to establish this medium as superior to traditionally printed materials in which methodology also stressed systematic phonics instruction.

The Linguistic (Regular Spelling) Approach

Of all the newer methods that emerged in the post-Flesch period, this one may well be the strangest. These materials were first published by Leonard Bloomfield in 1942. For the next decade, Bloomfield and his colleague Clarence L. Barnhart collaborated in efforts to have the materials adapted and used in mainstream reading instruction. However, during this time they received little if any favorable response or acceptance.

After Bloomfield's death and the increasing emphasis on teaching phonics, Barnhart published *Let's Read: A Linguistic Approach* in 1961. The materials contained therein had no roots in any branch of linguistic science. However, Bloomfield was a noted linguist and the term *linguistics* was popular and frequently invoked by critics of reading instruction. Thus the subtitle, *A Linguistic Approach.*

The irony of *Let's Read* is that it was published as part of the *Why Johnny Can't Read* revolution, the main thrust of which was the relentless, hard-nosed teaching of phonics or code cracking. Somehow, *Let's Read* was able to pose as code-cracking material even though the teaching of phonics or letter-sound relationships was proscribed.

The most tenable hypothesis as to how this could have happened was that the material so closely resembled a previously used phonics instructional approach that the two were confused. This was especially the case in regard to the systematic teaching of a series of words that each ended with the same phonogram. This was called the "word-family" approach, and the word families were identical to the spelling patterns stressed in the regular spelling approach. Some examples are *cat, hat, mat, fat, bat* and *can, man, tan, fan, ran.* The teaching methodologies involved in the two approaches, however, were antithetical. In the word-family method, children were taught to think and say the sound represented by the first letter. This sounding clue helped them distinguish between the sounds of the words c*at,* h*at,* m*at,* f*at,* b*at,* s*at,* p*at,* and r*at.* In the regular spelling methodology, children had to learn each word configuration by memory.

The Regular Spelling Instructional Program

Vocabulary control (regular spelling concept).   The major premise of these materials was that initial instruction should be based exclusively on a unique vocabulary-control principle. This principle was that in early reading instruction, the child should meet only those words that have "regular spellings," a term used to designate words in which printed letters represent "the most characteristic sound" associated with each letter.

The word *cat* would meet this criterion, but the word *cent* would be irregular because the *c* does not represent the characteristic *k* sound but rather the sound usually represented by *s.* The spelling of *bird* is irregular because the *i* represents a sound usually represented by *u* (burd) as does the *o* in *come* (kum).

Initial teaching (letter names, not letter sounds).   In the regular spelling approach, the child was taught letter recognition and letter names (aye, bee, see, dee, ee, eff). After the letters are learned in isolation they are combined into words:

> The child need not even be told that the combinations are words; and he should certainly not be required to recognize or read words. *All he needs to do is read off the names of the successive letters, from left to right.* (Bloomfield, 1961, p. 36)

Then the child is ready to begin working his way through a series of words that end with identical letter-phoneme patterns (*can, fan, man, tan*). Bloomfield (1961) suggested that teaching should proceed as follows.

1. Print and point to the word CAN.
2. The child is to read the letters "see aye en."
3. The teacher states "Now we have spelled the word. Now we are going to *read* it. This word is can. Read it *can."*
4. Present another word from the "an family" such as *tan.* (p. 41)

The aim of this teaching method was to have the child distinguish between various words that differ only in the initial grapheme-phoneme. However, the child was never taught the association between the initial letter and the sound it represents in words. There is no question but that a child must learn this relationship in order to become an independent reader.

Meaning waived in beginning instruction.   Unfortunately, many of the English words we use most frequently in building even the simplest of sentences have irregular spellings. Some examples include *a, the, was, once, of, any, could, love, too, their, do, said, one, who, some, only, gone, live, father, give, many, are, would, come, head, both, again, been, have, they, there, to, get,* and *should.* Typical English sentences are difficult to build when one decides to use only words that follow regular spelling patterns. For example, in Bloomfield's (1961) material, after the teaching of 66 words (roughly equivalent to several preprimers in a representative basal series), one finds only the most contrived sentences and absolutely no story line.

> Pat had ham.
> Nat had jam.
> Sam had a cap.
> Dan had a hat.
> Sam ran.
> Can Sam tag Pam?
> Can Pam tag Sam? (p. 65)

After 200 words had been learned, the child read these sentences.

> Let Dan bat.
> Did Al get wet?
> Van had a pet cat.
> Get up, Tad!
> Let us in, Sis!
> Sis, let us in!
> Let Sid pet a pup. (Bloomfield, 1961, p. 87)

If letter-sound relationships were learned, the child could then use this learning in future reading tasks. For instance, learning the sound that *b* represents in the word b*at* would transfer to the *b* in other word families such as b*et,* b*it,* b*ut,* b*ad,* b*ud,* b*id,* b*ug,* b*un,* b*us,* b*ag,* b*ig,* and b*ed.* More important, the knowledge of the sound *b* represents would also function in words with irregular spellings because the sound represented by *b* remains consistent in hundreds of these words (barn, ball, bath, bird, bold, busy, burn, both, bow).

Only 38% of the *Let's Read* program consisted of regularly spelled words. It is clear that what was learned in the initial instruction was not expected to transfer to the remaining two thirds of the program. Bloomfield (1961) revealed the Achilles heel of the material when he stated,

> "When it comes to teaching irregular and special words, each word will demand a separate effort and separate practice" (p. 206).

No guidelines or blueprint for such instruction was provided. Initial instruction soon exhausted the easier aspects of learning to read. Then children and teachers were abandoned when the more difficult aspects of learning to read could no longer be avoided.

The Individualized Reading and Language Experience Approaches

While the highly structured beginning reading programs just discussed were seeking converts, there also emerged a philosophy of reading instruction that sought to curtail or abolish much of the structure and routine associated with the basal programs. This new philosophy operated under the twin banner of the *Individualized Reading*

Movement and the *Language Experience Approach.* The chief premises of these new approaches included the following.

1. Reliance on basal reader materials was to be avoided. These were considered to be too restrictive, dull, and uninspiring.
2. Trade books (children's literature) were to be plentiful in every classroom.
3. Children were to select the reading materials they wished to read.
4. Both reading and writing were to be incorporated into the reading instruction curriculum. They were considered to be complementary parts of language acquisition.
5. Children were to write, or dictate to the teacher, their own experiences or stories. These reading materials were to remain available in the classroom as long as the materials had motivational value.
6. Teachers were to schedule a time period for any child who could profit from a teacher-pupil conference.
7. Workbooks and their repetitive teaching of skills were frowned upon.

This new emphasis on children reading children's literature was a significant departure from the turn of the century's emphasis on literature. Then, the focus had been on adult classics that had been authenticated by adults as having "cultural value." The emphasis on children's literature as an integral part of the reading-instruction curriculum was a significant development. This was a reform that contained the potential for an educational revolution.

WHOLE LANGUAGE

The individualized reading approach's break with traditional instruction and its emphasis on integrating writing and reading instruction became the foundation for the whole-language movement. Whole language is not an instructional program, and its proponents do not claim that it is. It has been called a philosophy, a dynamic system of beliefs, a child-centered curriculum, and a means for empowering children. Goodman (1992), describing the status of whole language, writes, "Whole language is producing a holistic reading and writing curriculum which uses real authentic literature and real books" (p. 196).

Both supporters and critics agree that the concept of whole language is vague. One is invited into a seemingly attractive territory for which there is as yet no map. Its position is reminiscent of descriptions of individualized reading made in the mid-1970s:

> Paradoxically its greatest potential strengths and weaknesses stem from the same factor. There is no concise definition of "what it is" and thus no blueprint for 'how to do it'. . . . In one sense, individualized reading focuses on the child-as-a-reader more than the teacher-as-a-teacher. (Heilman, 1977, pp. 306–308)

Goodman (1992) has written that "whole language aims to be an inclusive philosophy of education" (p. 196). Actually, it has not been totally inclusive. There is a litmus test that proscribes the direct teaching of *reading skills* (which is a codeword for *phonics*). This cannot be explained away as being a gratuitous diversion: It is the chief article of faith of true believers in whole language. Whole language can fit comfortably at every level of the curriculum except for the period called "learning to read." Here one must develop the skills needed to move into a literature curriculum.

Whole language is the latest version of that magnificent obsession that children might be successful in reading literature prior to solving the written code. What sustains this recurring dream? Is it based on the fact that learning the code is not a totally pleasant experience? Adult critics have noticed this as they observe children learning to read. When these adult, expert readers read, they are immersed in and sustained by the power and beauty of language. They say, "Let beginning reading be like this. Let beginning readers become involved with the beauty of language that resides in literature." To believe that this can occur, it is necessary to blur the difference between reading and learning to read. However, reading and learning to read are not synonymous. Learning to read is the price we pay in order to read literature.

Relative to this discussion, Jerome Bruner, a psychologist who helped develop the cognitive approach in the 1950s, made a significant observation and shared it with reading teachers. He said, "Learning to read is not a self-sustaining activity" (1972). He knew that learning to read is not the same activity that expert readers experience when they read. For learners, some of the joy is missing. The power and beauty of language is held hostage by the unknown words that interrupt the melody of language.

While learning to read may not be a self-sustaining activity, it is an activity that must be sustained until children make it to the next level, which is reading. Readers, by definition, can deal independently with the printed page. Children at all levels of reading ability will meet some words that they do not instantly recognize. But if they have mastered the code, they will be able to solve the identity of most of these words. Once children reach this point on the learning-to-read continuum, they are ready for the whole-language curriculum.

Chapter 3

PREREQUISITES FOR PHONICS INSTRUCTION

PHONOLOGICAL AWARENESS: THE FIRST PREREQUISITE FOR PHONICS INSTRUCTION

Children enter the world as auditory learners. Children who develop their language with normal hearing ability attend to sounds all around them: caregivers "oohing" and "ah-hing," as well as the ongoing repetition of songs, rhymes, and important names in their lives. This ongoing auditory language-rich stimulation is a necessary ingredient for developing phonological awareness. Phonological awareness is the ability to think about all the possible sounds in a word: syllables, onset, rime, and phonemes. For example, the word "crack" can be heard as a one syllable word: crack. Crack can also be heard in its onset and rime form: cr-ack. Or crack can be heard as individual phonemes: c-r-a-ck.

Early in a child's development, phonological awareness occurs subconsciously. As the child learns language, he or she will subconsciously play with syllables (ma-ma, da-da), onsets and rimes (Holly, bolly, dolly, molly, wolly) and phonemes—usually with the loudest or last sound (hat,t,t,t,t). As the child becomes more phonologically aware, the play becomes more purposeful and the child develops an understanding that:

- words can rhyme.
- words can have one or more syllables.
- words are in sentences.
- words can begin and end with the same sounds.
- words are made up of small sounds called phonemes (this is the beginning of phonemic awareness).

There are many informal, play-like language activities that can purposely help children to analyze and articulate the sounds heard in their world. These activities should be orally directed and initiated—it is not necessary to have any print available.

1. Sound Ordering Activity

- The teacher determines three common sounds to make in the classroom. These sounds need to be familiar to the students (ringing bell, blowing whistle, knocking on the door).
- Ask the students to listen and watch carefully as you make each sound and name the object that makes the sound.
- Explain to the students that they will be asked to close their eyes and listen for the sounds. The goal is to try to listen carefully so that all students can recall the order that the sounds were made.
- Ask the students to close their eyes. You make the three sounds.
- Students open their eyes and try to recall the sounds in order.
- Guide their response by using three blank post-it™ notes (sound notes) arranged in a line on the board. Which sound do they recall hearing? They recall hearing the bell. Was that the first sound, the middle sound, or the final sound? By using these prompts, you are helping the students to develop an ordering skill that will be very helpful when analyzing sounds (phonemes) in words for phonemic awareness.
- Once the students have ordered the sounds, you can draw simple illustrations on the post-it notes.
- Ask a student to point to each post-it note as you make the sounds.

Extension Activity: On another day, ask a student to secretly reorder the post-it notes. These notes should be kept out of sight from the remainder of the class. You direct the class as detailed previously. Place new blank post-it notes (sound notes) on the board. Make the sounds as determined by the student. The goal is to have the remaining members of the class determine the new order of sounds. The student selected to secretly reorder the sounds receives guided support from you in determining if the students can recall the correct order.

Further Extensions: While out on a walk, stop and listen to the sounds for a few moments. Try to order the first three sounds you hear during that brief pause.

2. Word Ordering Activity

Say a familiar short poem to the students. For example, say the following,

> "Peas porridge hot
> Peas porridge cold,
> Peas porridge in the pot
> Nine days old."

- Ask the students to recite it after you.
- Tell the students, "I want you to listen carefully to the first line of the poem: 'Peas porridge hot.' Repeat it after me. What is a word that you remember saying? Was that the first word, second word or last word?"

- Place three blank post-it notes (word notes) on the board and point to them saying, "Peas porridge hot." Help the students to locate the post-it note (word note) that corresponds to the word they remember hearing.
- Once all the words have been recalled and ordered, recite and say "Peas porridge hot" together and point to the post-it notes as you say the words. (Remember, this is an auditory activity so print is not necessary. You are helping the students to recall a three-word phrase, order the three words, and see the words as distinct sounds in the phrase.)

Extension Activity: Develop a three or four-word sentence about school. This can be done together as a class activity.

- Once you have come up with the sentence, place post-it notes on the board as you recite the sentence together. For example, "We like recess."
- Recite the sentence together and point to the blank post-it notes in correct sentence order, moving from left to right as you say each word.
- Ask the students to point to the post-it note that represents "We." This is called the first word. Ask them to point to the note for "recess." This is the second word. What post-it note represents "recess?" What would we call that word? This is the third word.
- Count the words and read the sentence together once again.

3. Direction Ordering Activity

List three simple directions that involve a series of tasks. For example, explain to the students that when they enter the classroom each day, they must sign-in at their table, pull out their notebooks, and select a book for silent reading.

- Place three post-it notes (direction notes) on the board.
- Ask the students to recall one of the directions.
- Is it the first direction, the second direction, or the last direction?
- Work at recalling the other directions and ordering them.
- Once the directions have been recalled and ordered correctly, recite them together.
- Draw simple illustrations on the post-it notes to help the students recall the directions as prompts for their independent work time.

4. Rhyming Activity: Beginning Play with Onsets and Rimes

Immerse the students in rich poetry and song that is filled with rhyming words. Talk about the words that have an ending (rime) that sounds the same. Play with these words by placing beginning sounds on the end and determining if these are sensible words or nonsense words. For example, "Miss Mary Mack" is a wonderful rhythmic poem that can be used to illustrate this activity. Say it several times with the students so that they are familiar with the poem and can easily recite it with you.

> "Miss Mary Mack, Mack, Mack
>
> All dressed in black, black, black
>
> With silver buttons, buttons, buttons,
>
> All down her back, back, back."

- After reciting it a number of times, ask the following: What words in this poem have the same ending sound? (As much as possible, give the students appropriate thinking time so that these responses are student-generated and teacher-guided.) For example, mack, black, back. These words rhyme.
- Now, listen carefully to how these words sound together: Mack, buttons. What do you notice about these words? (They do not rhyme. Their ending sounds are different.)
- Let's make other words that rhyme with Mack, black and back. (Again, give the students appropriate thinking time so that these responses are student-generated and teacher-guided.) For example, tack, sack, gack.
- Is tack a real word that makes sense and sounds right? Have you ever heard of a tack?
- Is sack a real word that makes sense and sounds right? Have you ever heard of a sack?
- Is gack a word that makes sense and sounds right? Have you ever heard of a gack?

5. Ordering Words into Sentences Activity

Select sentences from rhythmic, familiar, patterned reading text. For example, a sentence that appears repeatedly in a familiar book that the students know well: "The people ran and ran!"

- Read the sentence and place post-it notes (word notes) on the board (one for each word).
- Recite the sentence together and point to the post-it notes (word notes).
- Ask the students to count the post-it notes and determine how many words are in the sentence.
- Locate the first word and say it.
- Locate the last word and say it.
- Change the text to include an animal name. "The horses ran and ran."
- Locate which post-it note will represent "horses."
- Locate the post-it notes that represent "ran."
- Change the word "ran" to "ate." "The horses ate and ate."
- Locate "horses."
- Locate "ate and ate."

6. Syllable Activity

Gather the students in a circle on the floor. Using the children's names, clap the number of syllables in each child's name as you say it. This can be done in a round-like fashion.

- As you clap his or her name, give each student the correct number of note cards to correspond to the number of syllables in his or her name.
- These cards are placed on the floor in front of them and are used as syllable prompts for clapping syllables the second time around.
- After all the names have been clapped and each child has the correct number of note cards, softly work around the circle saying their names, clapping the syllables and counting the note cards. For example:

  "Sar-ah." Clap, clap. Two syllables.

  "Sam." Clap. One syllable.

  "Ro-ber-ta." Clap, clap, clap. Three syllables.

- Take time to discuss the idea that all words and names can have one syllable, two syllables, three syllables, or more.

Extension Activity: Take the cards and sort them on a bulletin board according to those names that have one syllable, two syllables, three syllables, etc. These can be arranged in a chart-like fashion with a small photograph of each child next to his or her corresponding syllable note cards. Students are encouraged to take a pointer and count, or clap, the syllables on their own.

7. Onset and Rime Activity

As with all the above activities, the following will continue to be auditory-based with no use of letters or words. The goal of all these activities is the ongoing discussion about sounds: the type of sound (sound in the room, words in a phrase, words in a sentence, or syllables in a word), the location of the sound (first, middle, or last), and what makes that sound (object, word, syllable). This next activity reflects a higher level of phonological awareness: onsets and rimes.

- This activity can be used with poetry, songs, names, and environmental print. It is recommended to select a one-syllable word that can have several possibilities of sensible onsets. For example, if you have a student in your classroom with the name "Pam," use her name. You can also bring in a piece of environmental print that has a familiar one-syllable label: CREST.
- Say "Pam" and clap out the syllables (one clap).
- Explain that you are going to listen for smaller sounds in Pam's name and that you are most interested in using her name to rhyme with other words.
- Place two post-it notes (sound notes) on the board and say P-AM. Point to the first note for /P/, and the second note for /AM/. Remind the students that you are talking about something different than syllables.
- Ask the students to locate the note for /P/. Is this the first sound or the last sound in PAM?

- Ask the students to locate the note for /AM/. Is this the first or last sound?
- Point to the /AM/ post-it note. What is this again? Can you think of any words that would rhyme with the /AM/ sound in PAM?
- As students come up with words, slowly sound them out accordingly: S-AM, H-AM, SL-AM, J-AM. While you do this, point to the correct blank post-it notes. If a student responds with a word that does not share the rhyme, but shares the onset /P/, point out that they are hearing the first sound in PAM.

8. Phoneme Activity: Preparation for phonemic awareness

Using a familiar one-syllable, three-sound word, place three post-it notes on the board. These must be arranged in left to right progression, with a small space between each note. It is important to select a word that is familiar to the students: a student's name, a familiar word from a song, poem or text, or environmental print. For example, if you have read a familiar text about a CAT, this would be an excellent word to select.

- I would like to take some time to talk about the smallest sounds in CAT. CAT has a syllable sound. Let's clap it. CAT. CAT has one syllable.
- CAT has two smaller sounds that we can hear as /C/ /AT/. These are the two sounds in CAT that we can use to make silly words and real words for rhyming play.
- CAT also has three very small sounds. Let's see if we can hear any of the smallest sounds in CAT.
- Listen and watch as I point to our sound notes (post-it notes) and then we will talk about what you remember hearing.
- Say /C/ softly and carefully, and point to the first note, /A/ and point to the middle note, /T/ and point to the final post-it note. (Be very careful to say the sounds softly and not stretch them out into a syllable formation. It is helpful to whisper the sounds and try to keep them as short as possible.)
- What sound do you remember hearing? (Please give the students appropriate thinking time so that these responses are student-generated and teacher-guided.) Did you say that you heard a /T/?
- Where do you think you heard it in the word CAT? Point to the notes and say /C/ softly, and point to the first note, /A/ and point to the middle note, /T/ and point to the final post-it note. Can you tell which sound note is the /T/ sound?
- Now locate the next sound (most often the /C/). Unless you have a speller in your classroom, the vowel sound will not be discriminated by most of your students. Talk about how hard it can be to hear this sound and describe it and locate it as the middle sound.
- Say all the sounds in order and point to the post-it notes (sound notes).
- Play this activity several times a week with fun, meaningful words.

PHONEMIC AWARENESS: THE SECOND PREREQUISITE FOR PHONICS INSTRUCTION

A second important prerequisite for phonics instruction is phonemic awareness. This term refers to the knowledge or understanding that speech consists of a series of sounds and that individual words can be divided into phonemes. Phonemic awareness is the ability to identify and manipulate these sounds (phonemes). Once a child develops an awareness of the smallest sounds in a word, he or she is able to understand that:

- words have small sounds that can be pulled apart and put back together.
- sounds in words have a specific order (first sound, middle sound, final sound).
- sounds in words can be counted.
- sounds in words can be moved, removed or replaced to make new words.
- several sounds can be presented represented with many different letters.

DEVELOPING PHONEMIC AWARENESS

In learning speech, individual phonemes are slighted. Preschool children have developed expertise in differentiating words as speech units. They tend to hear syllables and shorter words as auditory wholes. That is, when they hear or say the word *stand,* they are unaware that what they say or hear is speech-flow consisting of a blend of five speech sounds (phonemes). In order to learn to read the printed code, they must become proficient in segmenting syllables into their constituent phonemes. This ability has been found to be an accurate predictor of success in early reading achievement.

There are many instructional procedures that can enhance children's development of phonemic awareness. Regardless of their educational experience, children will learn and progress at vastly different rates. It is no longer questioned that the earlier children master this skill, the more rapid is their progress in learning to read.

Phonemic awareness skills are rarely well developed while children are learning speech prior to entering school. These skills should be taught both before and along with early reading instruction. They are developmental in nature, which suggests that regardless of what has been mastered, there is more to be learned. The following are oral language activities that do not involve children with print.

HEARING SPEECH SOUNDS IN WORDS

1. Explain that words are made up of one or more sounds. Inquire if anyone can name a word that has only one sound. Eventually choose *I* as a word that has only one sound. Have children pronounce *I*.

   "Now I say the word *hi.* How many sounds in *hi*?

   Yes, we hear two sounds in *hi,* one sound in *I.*

   The sound *a* is a word in a sentence like 'There is *a* cow!'

   Do cows eat *a*? What do cows eat?

   Yes, cows eat *hay.*

   Do you hear two sounds in *hay*?"

   (If someone interjects that there are three letters in the word *hay,* congratulate her and agree, but point out we *hear* just two speech sounds (*h/a/*).

   Variation: "How many sounds do we hear in the word *zoo*?

   Yes, two in *zoo.*

   How many in *zoom*?

   in *moo*?

   in *moon*?

   Children may enjoy a little doggerel.

   Two in *zoo,* three in *zoom.*

   Still two in *moo,* and three in *moon.*

   But four we hear when we say *spoon!*"

2. Same or Different

   Pronounce pairs of words. In some pairs, have both words contain the same number of speech sounds. In other pairs, have the words differ in the number of speech sounds they contain. Children respond "*same*" or "*different*" following each pair.

owl - fowl (d)	rain - train (d)	come - hum (s)
ask - try (s)	go - sun (d)	jump - fire (d)
goose - moose (s)	sled - flag (s)	nail - snail (d)
play - say (d)	sled - led (d)	spot - stop (s)

3. Next Difficulty Level

   Use the same or similar data found in Activity 2. Pronounce each pair of words. Children identify the number of speech sounds heard in each word, i.e., "Four sounds in *sled;* three sounds in *led.*"

   Variation: "I will say two words. Only one of them will be made up of three speech sounds. Repeat the word that has three sounds."

3	3	3	3
(too — took)	(see — set)	(sat — at)	(ate — hat)
3	3	3	3
(hid — he)	(fast — man)	(seek — sheep)	(stop — play)

INITIAL SOUNDS IN WORDS

1. Children listen to the pronunciation of a series of words, all of which begin with the same sound: *make, most, must, made, mine, meet.* Children then volunteer other words that begin with the /m/ sound: *mile, music, month, mail, mop, mask.*

2. Collect a number of pictures from workbooks, catalogues, or magazines. Select several pairs of pictures whose naming words begin with the same sound. Attach each picture to a separate piece of cardboard to make handling easier. Children then group pictures according to their initial sound (ball-boat; house-horse; fence-feather; pig-pumpkin; log-ladder). As the children progress, the difficulty level of the exercise can be increased by including three or more pictures whose names begin with the same sound. Of course, the objects in the pictures should be known by the children.

3. Rimes in search of an onset.

   Review: In the word *cap,* c is the onset; *ap* is the rime.

   Explain that each sentence you read will end with two speech sounds that do not make a word. Children are to add one sound in front of these sounds to make a word.

   Examples: "He was chewing _um." Children say, "*Gum.*"

   "The car was stuck in the _ud." Children say, "*Mud.*"

How fast can he _un?	(r)
A baby goat is a _id.	(k)
The boys name is _om.	(T)
False hair is a _ig.	(w)
Never play with a _un.	(g)
That pot has no _id.	(l)
The guide looked at the _ap.	(m)
He caught the fish in a _et.	(n)
The light was very _im.	(d)
The squirrel ate the _ut.	(n)

   Variation: "Add a sound in front of the word I pronounce to make a new word."

   at converts to (b*at,* r*at,* h*at,* p*at,* m*at*)

   an converts to (f*an,* m*an,* t*an,* r*an,* c(k)*an*)

it converts to (h*it*, l*it*, p*it*, w*it*, s*it*)

am converts to (j*am*, d*am*, h*am*, S*am*)

in converts to (w*in*, f*in*, t*in*, b*in*, s*in*)

all converts to (b*all*, c*all*, h*all*, f*all*, t*all*)

eat converts to (h*eat*, b*eat*, m*eat*, s*eat*, n*eat*)

4. Delete the initial sound and make a new word.

"I will say a word. If you say all but the first sound in that word, you will make a different word."

Examples: If I say *cup,* you say _____ ? up

If I say *bus,* you say _____ ? us

Teacher		Student						
pan	-	an	hit	-	it	beat	-	eat
win	-	in	ham	-	am	hand	-	and
can	-	an	spin	-	pin	tin	-	in
sand	-	and	small	-	mall	spill	-	pill
twin	-	win	howl	-	owl	jam	-	am

WORKING WITH RHYMES

The purpose of the following activities is to provide practice in discriminating speech sounds in words, specifically rhyming elements. In addition, the exercises focus on developing other skills such as listening (limiting responses to one category: e.g., numbers, colors, or animals), following directions, and noting stress and intonation patterns.

1. Thinking of Rhyming Words

Explain that you are going to read some sentences. Children are to listen carefully so they can supply words that rhyme with the last word in each sentence. The last word in the sentence should be stressed; in some classroom situations, it may even be advisable to repeat it.

1. Be sure to wear a hat on your *head.* (red, bed, Ted, said)
2. We will take a trip to the *lake.*
3. John, you may pet the *cat.*
4. They all said hello to the *man.*
5. Have you ever seen a *moose?*
6. We watched the bird build its *nest.*
7. Let's all count to *ten.*
8. Mary walked in the rain and got *wet.*
9. Sunday, we went to the *beach.*

Variation: Prepare sentences in which the final word is omitted. In reading the sentence, emphasize one word. A child completes the sentence by giving a word that rhymes with the word that is emphasized. This procedure also teaches the concept of stress as part of intonation patterns.

1. A *frog* sat on a _____ . (log)
2. Mary will *bake* a chocolate _____ . (cake)
3. Please do not bounce the *ball* in the _____. (hall)
4. On his finger the *king* wore a _____ . (ring)
5. Kate will *wait* by the _____ . (gate)
6. Keith swept the *room* with a nice new _____ . (broom)

2. Number Rhymes

Explain that you will pronounce and emphasize two words that rhyme with a number word. The children are to supply the rhyming number word to finish each sentence.

1. *Blue* and *shoe* rhyme with _____ . (two)
2. *Gate* and *hate* rhyme with _____ . (eight)
3. *Fix* and *mix* rhyme with _____ . (six)
4. *Drive* and *hive* rhyme with _____ . (five)
5. *Gun* and *run* rhyme with _____ . (one)
6. *Tree* and *see* rhyme with _____ . (three)
7. *When* and *then* rhyme with _____ . (ten)
8. *Pine* and *line* rhyme with _____ . (nine)
9. *Door* and *more* rhyme with _____ . (four)
10. *Eleven* and *heaven* rhyme with _____ . (seven)

To provide practice in speaking in sentences, have one volunteer say the entire sentence after each rhyme: "*Gate* and *late* rhyme with *eight.*"

Variation: This activity is similar to the preceding one except that the last word you speak is the clue to the rhyming word.

Teacher: "Give me a number that rhymes with _____ ."

1. *fun* (one)
2. *fix* (six)
3. *fine* (nine)
4. *floor* (four)
5. *bee* (three)
6. *hen* (ten)
7. *late* (eight)
8. *do* (two)
9. *alive* (five)
10. *heaven* (seven)

3. Color Names to Complete a Rhyme

Teacher: "Name the color that rhymes with _____ ."

1. *head* and *bed* (red)
2. *clean* and *queen* (green)
3. *tray* and *play* (gray)
4. *do* and *you* (blue)
5. *track* and *back* (black)
6. *town* and *gown* (brown)
7. *man* and *ran* (tan)

8. *sight* and *kite* (white)
9. *think* and *sink* (pink)
10. *fellow* and *Jell-O* (yellow)

4. Animal Names to Complete a Rhyme

Teacher: "Name an animal that rhymes with _____ ."

1. *hat* (rat, cat)		**6.** *near* (deer)	
2. *log* (dog, frog)		**7.** *jeep* (sheep)	
3. *house* (mouse)		**8.** *cantaloupe* (antelope)	
4. *boat* (goat)		**9.** *big* (pig)	
5. *mitten* (kitten)		**10.** *box* (fox)	

5. Rhyming Words and Following Directions

Each participant should have two 3" × 5" cards with the word *yes* printed on both sides of one card, and *no* printed on both sides of the other. Read statements similar to those below. If the two emphasized words rhyme, children hold up the *yes* card; if the words to not rhyme, they hold up the *no* card.

a. I say *fox* and *box*. (yes)
b. I say *coat* and *road*. (no)
c. I say *found* and *ground*. (yes)
d. I say *man* and *men*. (no)
e. I say *car* and *cart*. (no)
f. I say *feet* and *meet*. (yes)
g. I say *book* and *look*. (yes)
h. I say *glass* and *dress*. (no)
i. I say *bug* and *rug*. (yes)
j. I say *chair* and *church*. (no)

6. Forming Rhymes with Letter Names

Teacher: "Name a letter (or letters) that rhymes with _____ ." Or, "What letter(s) rhymes with _____ ?"

1. *say* and *day* (a, k, j)
2. *me* and *tree* (b, c, d, e, g, v, t, z, p)
3. *sell* and *bell* (l)
4. *hen* and *ten* (n)
5. *high* and *sky* (i, y)
6. *far* and *car* (r)
7. *true* and *blue* (u, q)
8. *them* and *gem* (m)
9. *no* and *grow* (o)
10. *dress* and *less* (s)

HEARING FINAL SOUNDS IN WORDS (NON-RHYMING)

Besides practice on initial sounds and rhyming elements, children need auditory practice in matching and differentiating the final sound in words (nonrhyming elements). It is easier for children to note that *cat* and *rat* end with the same sounds than it is to note that *cat* and *tent* end with the same sound.

1. Pairs of Words

Pronounce pairs of words, some of which end with the same sound. If the two words end with the same sound, the children respond "same"; if the final sounds are different, they say "different."

1. *net* and *but* (same)
2. *fan* and *fat* (different)
3. *fog* and *pig* (same)
4. *hen* and *man* (same)
5. *six* and *tax* (same)
6. *bus* and *gas* (same)
7. *hat* and *hid* (different)
8. *leg* and *let* (different)
9. *rub* and *rug* (different)
10. *lip* and *tap* (same)
11. *hop* and *hot* (different)
12. *log* and *bug* (same)

 MOM AND POP WORDS

Invite children to listen carefully as you pronounce a number of words. Explain that some of these words will begin and end with the same sound while others will not.

Examples: *pup* "Does *pup* begin and end with the same sound?" (yes)

  bed "Does *bed* begin and end with the same sound?" (no)

"Now, when I say a word, you repeat it. If the first and last sounds are the same, say *yes*. If they are not the same, say *no*."

tent (yes)	tube (no)	soon (no)	toast (yes)	did (yes)
dad (yes)	pep (yes)	mom (yes)	bud (no)	trip (no)
noon (yes)	top (no)	pep (yes)	toot (yes)	pop (yes)

 DELETE A FINAL PHONEME (THE WORD YOU MAKE IS ?)

Select a series of words that form a different word when the last sound is deleted. Children listen carefully as each word is pronounced. Then they repeat all but the last sound, which results in a different word.

Examples: If I say *card*, you say _____ . (car)

When I say *seem*, you say _____ . (see)

and (an)	farm (far)	tent (ten)	howl (how)	Anna (Ann)	seek (see)
boot (boo)	meat (me)	ant (an)	farms (farm)	start (star)	mend (men)
wind (win)	wasp (was)	zoom (zoo)	seal (sea)	hump (hum)	team (tea)

There are many ways to help children develop phonemic awareness. Some that are experienced by children before they enter school are continued well into reading instruction. These include contact with nursery rhymes, children's songs, alphabet books and songs, children's educational TV, and Dr. Seuss and other "I-Can-Read" books.

VISUAL DISCRIMINATION: THE THIRD PREREQUISITE FOR PHONICS INSTRUCTION

Children will have had innumerable experiences in making visual discriminations before they enter school and are called upon to make the much finer discriminations required in reading. The school will then provide many readiness activities that foster visual discrimination skills. Some of these may be only vaguely related to learning to read—matching objects and geometric forms, noting missing parts of pictures, and the like.

Other activities will relate more closely to the tasks required in reading. Studies have established that the ability to name the letters of the alphabet is one of the best predictors of a child's success in beginning reading. However, naming letters is a memory-association skill and is really not the crucial issue. The importance of being able to name letters is that it establishes that the child can discriminate visually among the various letter forms. Children have an almost uncanny ability to learn names or labels. Thus, teaching letter names is not the primary goal, but the ability to name letters is the criterion for establishing visual discrimination of graphic forms.

 ## MATCHING AND NAMING LETTER FORMS

1. Match Letters

Duplicate exercises similar to the following illustration. The children circle or trace each letter on the line that is exactly like the stimulus on the left.

C	C	O	Q	O
g	d	g	b	g

2. Flash Card Drill

a. Prepare large flash cards for each letter of the alphabet. Hold up a card and select a volunteer to name the letter or have the group name the letter in unison.

b. Prepare smaller letter-cards for each participant with the same letter form on the front and back of the card.

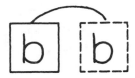

Hand out identical card groups of three or four to all participants, who spread the cards on their desks. Give directions: "Hold up the letter *m.*" Observe children who are having difficulty and provide added practice for these students.

3. Build a Pile

a. This is a game for two or more children. Use a pack of letter cards, each of which has a letter form on one side only.

b. The cards are placed face down and the first player draws a card. He shows the card, and if he names the letter he places it face down in his pile.

c. When a player fails to name the letter, the next player may try to name it and place it in her pile. Then she draws a card.

d. At the end of the game, the player with the most cards wins.

4. Two-letter Sequence

Duplicate a series of two-letter words. Instruct children to circle each word that is exactly like the stimulus at the left.

it		at	in	up	it
on		of	on	no	on
is		as	us	is	so

5. Three-letter Sequence

For added difficulty, use the same directions as for two-letter sequence using three-letter words.

sat		hat	sat	say	sad
can		cat	pan	can	cap
dug		dug	bug	dog	dug

MATCHING CAPITAL AND LOWERCASE LETTERS

1. The children draw a line from the capital letter at the left of the box to the matching lowercase letter at the right of the box.

A------a b a e	B b c p	E a m e
G g n r	H d g h	R d r f

2. Duplicate a page of boxes, each containing two letter forms. The children circle each pair of letters that contains both a capital and lowercase form of the same letter.

Hh	Ee	Fg	Bb
Ba	Gg	Dd	Aa

3. Prepare a series of cards similar to those used for the Flash Card Drill. (Each participant has lowercase letter cards for each letter in the exercise.) Place one capital letter form on the chalk tray. Call on a volunteer to place the matching lowercase letter below the capital form shown. Continue through the cards.

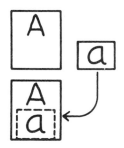

4. **a.** Duplicate Tic-Tac-Toe pages of squares composed of three-by-three smaller squares.

   b. Each set should have a capital letter in the center square and a variety of lowercase letters in all other squares. These should be arranged so that one line contains the capital and two lowercase forms of the same letter.

c. Have the children draw a line through the three squares that contain the same letter form.

TRACING LETTER FORMS

1. Print a large letter form on the chalkboard. Trace the form and say the letter name while children trace the form in the air and repeat the letter name.

2. Prepare duplicated pages showing a heavy-line letter form on the left and dotted letter outlines on the balance of the line. Children trace over the dots to form the letters.

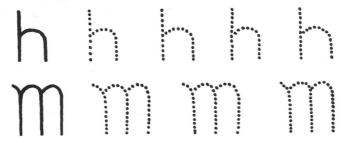

3. Duplicate a page of letter stimuli as shown. The children trace each letter outline that will result in the same letter as the stimulus at the left.

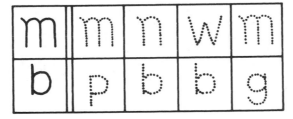

4. Prepare duplicated pages of letters as shown. After tracing the first letter outlined, the children print the letter in each of the remaining boxes on the line.

5. Prepare a page of letter symbols, each of which is followed by a partially completed letter. The children are to add the part that is missing in order to complete the letter shown at the left.

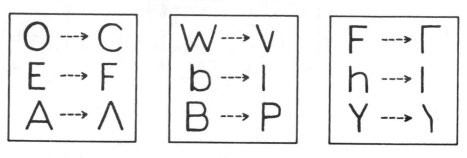

DISCRIMINATION OF WORD FORMS

In this task, children do not have to be able to name the words; they simply underline every word in the box that is the same as the stimulus word at the left. Exercises progress from gross differences to minimum differences.

lake	small	the	lake	name
word	take	word	each	word

ball	ball	fill	bat	ball
come	call	come	come	love

cat	can	cat	rat	cat
hand	band	sand	hand	hand

SUMMARY

This chapter focused on developing skills essential for beginning phonics instruction. These include developing phonemic awareness through activities such as counting speech sounds heard in words, isolating initial and final consonant sounds, adding and deleting phonemes to produce different words, and working with rhymes. Additionally, exercises focusing on building skills in visual discrimination of letter and word forms were presented.

Chapter 4

MOVING INTO READING

*W*hat do children bring to school that the school can build on in teaching beginning reading? The majority of children entering school are unabashed learning machines. They love challenges and are willing to grow. Prior to school, their most important intellectual achievement has been the mastery of language. Children can speak thousands of different words that are extremely close in pronunciation. They do not confuse words they hear that exhibit only the smallest phonemic differences. This achievement in acquiring language and concepts is of paramount importance in children's learning to read.

This points up a dilemma for educators. It is difficult to convince critics that both *learning* to read and *teaching* reading are difficult and frustrating experiences. Part of the problem is that educators are willing to stipulate that (a) reading is "getting meaning," (b) would-be readers come to school with a wealth of language meanings and concepts, and (c) beginning readers will not be asked to read materials that contain concepts beyond their grasp.

There is no doubt that mastery of language is the key to success in all future educational activities. Language is the tool of the school and the only magic available to teachers. However, the magic of language that is enjoyed by skilled readers is held to a minimum in the early stages of learning to read. It is held hostage until children have made significant progress in becoming independent readers. This level of proficiency is not achieved until children have developed the ability to identify words not instantly recognized.

Upon entering school, children know the meanings embedded in all of the material they will be expected to read in grades one and two. Yet they are unable to read a simple sentence in a book that contains no more than fifteen different words. If one should eavesdrop in first grade reading classes, he will never hear children ask, "What do these words mean?" They already know. Their question is, "What are these words?"

This question refers to printed words. Translate the print to speech and the child has no problem. Assume that on the first day of school, the first-grade teacher points to a word in a story and asks a nonreader, "What is this word?" Obviously, the child cannot answer. If the teacher says, "I will read you the sentence leaving out that word. Listen carefully and then tell me the word" and then reads, "The teacher asked the new girl, 'What is your _____?' " probably 95% of first-grade nonreaders could supply the missing word. This illustrates what nonreaders bring to school that relates to reading. Children are adequately equipped to deal with the language-meaning aspect of reading. However, they are helpless in the face of print until they have established what spoken words these strange visual symbols represent.

CONTRASTING LEARNING TO SPEAK AND LEARNING TO READ

If speaking were the only communication skill children had to learn, the process of schooling would be much easier. Learning to speak, for most children, is so easy, so rapid, so uncomplicated that it arouses awe among learning specialists. Debate on this phenomenon moves in circles:

> "It's a miracle that any child learns to speak so fluently so rapidly."
> "Wait! Acquiring speech is so universal it couldn't be a miracle!"
> "Universal—yes, *that's* the miracle."

In acquiring speech, children immediately become immersed in a meaning-making process. They learn individual words—some of which function as sentences. Children are able to articulate practically all of the phonemes in their language, yet they are lacking in phonemic awareness. They are unaware of having uttered three phonemes in pronouncing *June* and nine phonemes in saying *September.* In speech, the whole word is much more than the sum of its parts (phonemes). Children might choose speechlessness if forced to deal extensively with phonemes as a prelude to acquiring speech. This is why children make rapid growth in learning speech.

In essence, children learned speech by listening to speakers speak. Next, they imitated or repeated what they heard and were constantly rewarded for every effort at speech. The essential difference between learning speech and learning to read is that children cannot learn to read solely by listening to readers read. This is not to imply that modeling of good reading is not important in teaching emergent readers essential reading skills. Adults' reading to children is one of the most important influences on children's progress in learning to read.

CONTEXT CLUES

When a child is reading for meaning, the context in which he meets an unknown word is useful in suggesting what the word might be. Usually, only a few words could possibly "fill out" the meaning. For example:

The boy threw the ball to his _____ .

Probably fewer than a dozen words could logically be inserted in the blank space (friend, dog, mother, playmate, sister, father, brother). Some possibilities would be less logical than others depending on what has happened in the story prior to this sentence.

Writers use a number of devices to provide context clues that help readers identify new words and difficult concepts. One of these is to incorporate a description-definition in the text.

> They were now traveling through _____ country. It was very hot, there was sand underfoot, and the wind blew sand in their eyes. There were no streams— no water whatsoever—and no shade trees. The _____ extended as far as the eye could see.

Other context clues include comparison, contrast, and the use of synonyms and antonyms.

> At this point the stream flowed very _____ [rapidly]. The water splashed over the rocks and sent up white spray as it moved swiftly through the pass.

Solving the identity of an unknown word is facilitated by understanding the meaning of the sentence in which the words occurs as well as by understanding what has occurred in previously read sentences and sentences that follow—assuming, of course, that the child is reading for meaning.

In the first incomplete sentence above, the reader is restricted to context alone.

> "The boy threw the ball to his _____ ."

In a reading situation, one would not be confronted by a blank space, but by a series of letters. Notice that, when the reader heeds the initial letter and solves the sound it represents, the number of logical choices is drastically reduced:

> "The boy threw the ball to his s_____ ."

For most readers, this minimal clue will suffice. If not, one must proceed through the first syllable *sis* _____ .

HOW CHILDREN LEARN TO READ

The ease most children experience in learning speech is not always replicated in learning to read. Here children are confronted with a task that is totally foreign to any of their preschool experiences. Now they must learn to associate twenty-six visual symbols (letters) with the forty-four speech sounds they have learned to string into words and sentences when speaking.

Prior to entering school, most children have had some experience with letters of the alphabet, with alphabet books or blocks, and alphabet songs. Unfortunately, whatever experiences they have had will not prepare them for their next experience with the alphabet. Now they must crack the alphabetic code and learn the secrets of letter-sound relationships.

INTRODUCING PHONICS INSTRUCTION

Teachers should avoid undue loyalty to any instructional procedures including the illustrations offered here. A good rule is "adapt and improve—be comfortable." To illustrate one approach for teaching letter-sound relationships, the word *top* will be used. This word is in the children's speaking-listening vocabulary. They have acquired several meanings for *top,* including "a toy that spins," and "Clean off the top of your desk." Children will now meet the printed word and learn several concepts.

1. *Top* consists of three visual cues (letters).
2. Each letter represents a different speech sound.
3. When blended, these three sounds result in the pronunciation of the word *top.*
4. The sounds must be blended from left to right.
5. The sounds blended must not result in a *three-syllable word.* Thus, *top* cannot be sounded as *tee-oh-pe* or as the softer syllables *tuh-ah-puh.*

What then is the sound of /t/? It is the first sound one makes when pronouncing the word *top.* Say this to children and they may hear you, but it is likely to be processed as meaningless jargon.

How might they learn the sound of /t/? A chalkboard presentation to young learners might proceed as follows.

1. Print the word *top* on the board. Invite children to join in reading (saying) the word. Explain that the letter *t* tells us what the first sound will be when we say *top.* Add other words that begin with *t.* Point to and pronounce each word with the children, emphasizing or prolonging the /t/ sound.

Ask children to supply other words that begin with the /t/ sound. (t*ape,* t*wo,* t*est,* t*urn,* t*ax,* t*ruck,* t*ell,* t*old,* t*ime*)

2. *Onset in search of a rime.*

    Onset = the consonant(s) that precede the vowel(s) in syllables (including one-syllable words)
    Rime   = everything but the onset in syllables (including one-syllable words)

Example: top *t* = onset; *op* = rime

To help children distinguish the sound of the letter *t* in words, make a list of familiar words that begin with the sound of /t/. Pronounce and have children repeat each word in your list. (See Column A.)

Teacher: "I will start to say the first sound in *tag*. Before I finish, you say the rest of the word." (Column B) "Then we will repeat the word together." Follow the same procedure for each word in your list. Then reverse the procedure: children pronounce the onset /t/; teacher adds the rime.

A	B
tag	_ag
tent	_ent
time	_ime
toast	_oast
took	_ook

3. *Children bring t to the party.*

   This activity allows children to think, subvocalize, and mentally add the /t/ sound in front of words to form different words.

   Explain that you will pronounce a word, and children are to add the /t/ sound in front of that word. Then they pronounce the word they have created.

   Examples: If I say the word *able*

When you add the /t/ sound, you say	ta*ble*
If I say *all,* you would say	ta*ll*
If I say *rain,* you would say	t*rain*

   Print and pronounce the first word in Column A. Children add the /t/ sound and pronounce "their word" (Column B). Continue through all words in Column A.

A	B
each	t*each*
wig	tw*ig*
ask	ta*sk*
old	t*old*
ape	ta*pe*

   Other *t* words ____in, ____rust, ____oil, ____rip, ____an, ____ray, ____race, ____win
   Other initial consonants can be added to words to form new words.

   Examples:

b:	___all, ___rain, ___ox, ___and, ___rag, ___at, ___us
s:	___eat, ___ink, ___top, ___cat, ___and, ___he, ___hop
m:	___any, ___eat, ___ask, ___end, ___ink, ___old, ___an
p:	___in, ___aid, ___ill, ___rice, ___it, ___each, ___art

CONSONANT CONSISTENCY

Point out to children that there is a bonus each time they learn a letter-sound relationship. The sound represented by /t/ in *top* will be the same sound when it is met in thousands of other English words. This is true regardless of where *t* occurs in words. The *t* in *time, took, tune, hunt, cat, west, hunter, catcher* and *tomato* represents the same sound as heard in *top.*

Developing independence in reading progresses as instruction deals with letter sounds in final and medial positions. The final letter in *top* represents the same sound in *pen, pill, partnership, snap, paper, Pop, pup.* Other consonants that are highly consistent in the sound they represent include b — d — j — k — l — m — n — r — v.* The virtue of this consistency is that any instructional procedure will be equally effective in dealing with each of these letters.

BECOMING INDEPENDENT READERS

During the early months of grade one, learning the reading process is moving forward on all fronts. Other letter-sound relationships will have been explained and practiced. Children now have books that contain stories. They are frequently in contact with children's literature. In some classrooms, children are writing brief stories with little or no emphasis on correct spelling. In other classrooms, pupils tell stories that a teacher or aide writes down. These works are then read by their proud authors.

Along with progress there are setbacks and frustrations. For example, a child is reading a story that contains fewer than a dozen different words. The reader does not recognize the word *man* in the sentence, *"The man is sad."* The teacher suggests, "Sound it out." The child instantly responds, "Boy."

The peculiar thing about this situation is that the child heard the teacher and had the ability to do what was suggested. However, the child had already settled on a response that had worked before: guessing. In recent reading experiences, the child had met many words he did not instantly recognize and at various times had tried all of the following responses.

- Skipping the word
- Asking someone for help (teacher, parent, or peer)
- Ignoring all phonic clues and guessing the word
  (bad guess: makes no sense; the child then sounds it out)
  (good guess: correct word; reinforces guessing)
- Applying phonics to sound out the word
- Sounding out the first letter and instantly guessing the word
  (saying the wrong word: it makes sense; no problem)

*The teaching of vowel letter sounds is generally considered to be more difficult because vowels represent more than one sound as well as different sounds in different words. (See pp. 5-6 and Chapter 6.)

(saying the wrong word: it makes sense; big problem, because this time the substitute word demands changes later in the paragraph in order to keep the meaning)
- Trying to apply phonics, which doesn't work on the irregularly spelled word *once;* the child falls back on context clues, and solves the word
- Ad infinitum . . .

It is apparent that the beginning reader has many available options for solving unknown words. Some of these are very poor responses, but unfortunately, even the poorest are reinforced occasionally. Learning to read involves discarding ineffective responses and using all available clues that make for success. Examples of clues with very limited value would include unique letter configurations and pictures. The word *look* may be learned as having "two eyes" in the middle, but soon the child meets *book, took, stood, blood, good, boot* and *soon.* As children expand their reading, all of the so-called "unique features" (*oo, tt, ll,* final *y*) are found in more and more words, and thus become of less value in identifying words.

Pictures found in children's reading materials have motivational value and often can lure a child into reading. In some instances, pictures provide clues to unknown words (cliff, wagon, father, fireplace, bridge). Even so, it is obvious that pictures have limited value as a word identification tool.

Two clues that work very well with phonics are context clues and the structural characteristics of English.

STRUCTURAL CLUES

The earlier discussion of teaching the /t/ sound in *top* may have suggested that teaching individual letter sounds can be labor intensive. Perhaps one of the goals of reading instruction should be to produce learners who, in the words of Thomas Paine, "eventually become their own teacher." Children can move in this direction by acquiring insights into certain economies afforded by printed English. Sooner or later readers should discover that there are larger units of print within words that need not be dealt with letter-by-letter. Examples are prefixes such as pre–, dis–, trans–, sub–, un–, post–; and suffixes –tion, –ist, –less, –able, and –ness. After these have been met a number of times, to not treat them as units would be wasteful.

THE BLUE-COLLAR WORKING WORDS

There is another structural feature of English that impacts very early on learning to read. That is the fact that a hundred-plus high frequency words are used over and over in English speech and writing. These have been called "service words," "glue words," or "working words" because they literally hold the language together.

To illustrate this point, the brief preceding paragraph contains fifty-four words, twenty-seven of which are the working words under discussion. They are listed here in the order of their appearance above: *there, is, of, that, very, on, to, that, is, the, that, a, are, over, and, over, in, and, these, have, been, or, they, hold, the.*

Children reading text will rarely meet a sentence that does not contain one or more of these "working words," many of which are afflicted with irregular spellings. (*been, have, could, done, enough, the, are, of, they, once, said, would, some*). This drastically limits the help phonic analysis can provide. In essence, these words are either recognized instantly or they constantly interrupt the reading process. This, of course, disrupts the melody of language which is essential for meaningful reading.*

Teachers have received little advice on how to teach sight words most effectively. Perhaps this is because little is known about how children learn them. Possibly we overemphasize that instant recognition of words occurs more or less automatically as a result of frequent encounters with these words. All reading teachers can cite instances of children identifying high frequency words on a first encounter without subsequent recognition in later encounters.

If we knew more about how children learn sight words, would we be able to use that knowledge to teach children to read through visual discrimination alone? Decades ago, Smith (1973) posed a question that addressed the essence of the great debate over reading instruction:

> We can both recognize and recall many thousands of words in our spoken language vocabulary, and recognize many thousands of different faces and animals and plants and objects in our visual world. Why should this fantastic memorizing capacity suddenly run out in the case of reading? (p. 75)

The question Smith raises seems to invite the conclusion that visual memory of word configurations should be sufficient for learning to read. However, pedagogical experience has rendered the verdict that humans' fantastic memorizing capacity cannot be relied on to produce adequate readers.

Children can learn a number of sight words, but they cannot become skilled readers (even at the third-grade level) by relying exclusively on learning sight words. This is so because all printed words must be constructed (spelled) using a pool of only twenty-six visual (letter) symbols. Obviously, these few symbols must be used over and over in constructing all material printed in English. Many visual word forms begin to look very much alike because they *are* very much alike.

Although children should not rely on sight words alone to read skillfully, they should acquire a sight vocabulary. It is the skill that best illustrates the developmental nature of reading. Whenever a child is making normal progress in reading, his stock of sight words is increasing.

---

*Not counting the thirteen irregularly spelled words in parentheses, the paragraph above contains 65 words, of which 30 (46%) are "service" or working words. Your count may differ slightly because, as yet, we have no sacred list of these words.

SUMMARY

This chapter supports the premise that good reading instruction includes the right combination of word identification skills. To achieve optimum progress in learning to read, the would-be reader must acquire three compatible skills:

- Mastering and applying letter-sound relationships;
- Enlarging sight vocabulary; and
- Profiting from context clues while reading.

These skills are not to be achieved in the above order, or any other order. They function best when learned and applied concurrently.

This philosophy places phonics in proper perspective, reaffirming that it is neither a reading program or an optional additive. It is a partner that assumes its share of the responsibility for producing critical readers who, as they grow, will continue to love and revel in language.

5

CONSONANT LETTER-SOUND RELATIONSHIPS

*W*e have so far dealt with skills that are prerequisites for learning letter-sound relationships. The two major skills are the ability to discriminate among letter forms and the ability to differentiate auditorily among speech sounds as heard in words. This chapter will focus on teaching that combines these skills and leads children to associate a particular sound with a specific letter or combination of letters.

A WORD ABOUT SEQUENCE

The phonics program consists of teaching many specific skills. In any systematic program, this myriad of skills would have to be arranged into some teaching sequence. There are some options in regard to sequence that undoubtedly are of little educational consequence (such as whether to teach the sound of *t* before *b,* or *m* before *n*). On the other hand, the question of whether to teach consonant or vowel letter-sounds first is worthy of consideration.

Rationale for Teaching Consonant Sounds First

The majority of words children meet in beginning reading are words that begin with consonants. For instance, 175 (or approximately 80%) of the 220 words on the Dolch Basic Sight Word Test begin with consonants. The Dale List of 769 Easy Words contains an even higher proportion (87%) of words beginning with consonants.

It is good learning theory to have children start phonic analysis with the beginnings of words, working their way through the words from left to right. This reinforces the practice of reading from left to right and focuses children's attention on the first part of the word. This is essential for facile reading and an absolute prerequisite if children are to solve the word by sounding.

Consonants tend to be much more consistent than vowels in the sounds they represent. For instance, a number of consonants (*j, k, l, m, n, p, b, h, r, v, w*) represent only one sound. Certain other consonants that have two sounds present no problem in beginning reading instruction because one of the two basic sounds can be left until the child has had considerable practice in reading.

If a child uses skills in combination, sounding the initial consonant letter and using context-meaning clues will frequently be all the analysis that is needed. Assume each blank line in the following examples represents an unknown word.

1. _____ (This could represent any of 600,000 words in English.)
2. f_____ (Here, more than 98% of all words are eliminated. The unknown word must begin with the sound associated with the letter f.)

It is probable that the reader will arrive at the unknown word(s) in the following sentences despite the very limited context that is provided.

3. "You will have to pay the f_____ now," said the judge.
4. Without a doubt, pumpkin is my f_____ pie.
5. During J_____ it is much colder than it is in J_____ and J_____ .

The sequence of teachings suggested in this chapter follows.

1. Initial consonant letter-sounds
2. Initial consonant blends or clusters (bl, st, etc.)
3. Initial consonant digraphs (ch, wh, sh, th, etc.)
4. Final consonants, blends, and digraphs
5. Consonant irregularities

Listing this sequence does not imply that all the possible steps under 1 must be completed before introducing any of the teachings in 2, 3, 4, or 5. The procedures that follow illustrate some of the many approaches that can be used in teaching letter-sound relationships.

INITIAL CONSONANT LETTER-SOUNDS

One widely used technique for teaching initial letter-sounds is the use of children's names.

1. Write the names of several children in the class (or other common first names) that begin with the same letter (Bill, Beth, Ben, Brad) on the chalkboard.
2. Pronounce each name; then have the class pronounce each name.
3. Call attention to the fact that each name begins with the same letter, and that this letter (B) represents the same sound in each word.
4. Use other series of names for other letter-sounds.

Jason	Denise	Mary	Susan
Josh	Daniel	Matthew	Sam
Jill	Devon	Mike	Seth
Jamie	David	Maggie	Sarah

Other techniques for teaching initial letter-sounds follow.

1. **Chalkboard Drill**

   For purposes of illustration, we will give the steps for teaching the sound of the consonant *m* in detail. All other consonant sounds can be taught in the same manner.

   a. Print the letter *m* (capital and lowercase) on the chalkboard. Indicate that for the next few minutes the group will study the sound of the letter *m* as it is heard in words. Write on the board a column of previously studied words, all of which begin with the letter *m*. Any words the children have met (as sight words) in experience charts or other materials may be used—words such as *me, must, moon,* and *mind.* Also, familiar names and names of children in the class that call for capital letters may be used.

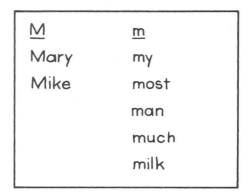

   b. Ask the children to look at the words carefully and name the letter that begins each word. Indicate that a big *M* or capital letter is used in names.

   c. As you pronounce the words, ask the children to listen to the sound heard at the beginning of each word. The initial sound should be emphasized, but not distorted.

   d. Invite children to read the words in unison, listening carefully to the sound of *m* as they say the words.

   e. Ask children to supply other words that begin with the sound /*m*/.

2. **Match a Pair**

   This game is an adaptation of Concentration; it involves the use of pictures and two or more children as participants (individual or team play).

   Select pairs of pictures so that two picture-naming words begin with the same letter-sound: h*orse*—h*and;* b*ell*—b*oat;* t*able*—t*ub;* f*ish*—f*ox;* and d*esk*—d*uck.* Shuffle the cards and lay them face down on the table.

   The first player turns up two cards, hoping to match a pair of initial letter-sounds. If the player is successful, she picks up both cards. If she does not match initial letter-sounds, both cards are again turned face down. Other players continue taking turns. Each player attempts to note and remember the location of pictures that have been turned up but not matched.

The winner is the player or team with the most pictures at the end of the game.

3. **Building a Picture Dictionary**

Use a supply of pictures from workbooks, magazines, and catalogues. Work with one letter at a time: *B—b,* for example.

After teaching the initial sound of *B—b* in words, have the children gather pictures whose naming words begin with that letter-sound. Children may work individually or in small groups.

Prepare a page (or several pages) for each letter-sound. Print a capital and lowercase letter at the top of the page and fill the page with pictures whose naming words begin with that letter-sound.

B - b

boot	bird	bed
bus	basket	book
barn	boat	boy

4. **Print and Sound**

Compile columns of easy words that begin with the letter-sounds to be taught or reviewed. Delete the initial letter of each word, and provide space for students to write the letter.

As they print the initial letter, the children pronounce the word they have formed. (Material may be presented on the chalkboard, with transparencies, or as duplicated exercises.) Here are several examples.

a. *Teacher:* "In each blank space, add the letter above the column of words. Pronounce each word."

t	*s*	*c*	*l*
____ ag	____ ad	____ ap	____ og
____ ub	____ ix	____ ot	____ ap
____ en	____ un	____ up	____ ed
____ op	____ it	____ an	____ eg
____ ip	____ ob	____ ub	____ et

b. *Teacher:* "In each blank space, write one of the letters *h, w,* or *g.* Be sure the letter you choose makes a word. Pronounce the word."

____ im	____ ot	____ ip	____ ub
____ et	____ un	____ ad	____ id
____ um	____ at	____ ig	____ ug
____ eb	____ en	____ ap	____ em

c. *Teacher:* "In each blank space, add any letter that will make a word."

____ ug	____ og	____ eg	____ at
____ ox	____ un	____ it	____ op
____ ad	____ ig	____ ub	____ in
____ en	____ an	____ ot	____ us

Mental Substitution

Day by day, in the early stages of reading instruction, the child is learning both sight words and the sounds of initial consonants. Knowledge thus gained can be applied in arriving at the pronunciation of other words not known as sight words. Assume the child knows the words *king* and *ring* and meets the unknown word *sing.* He should be able to combine the /s/ sound, which he knows in words like *sat, some,* and *say,* with the sound of *ing* found in *king* and *ring.* This involves a process of "thinking the sounds." To illustrate, let us assume the following:

1. A child has learned the italicized words in Table 5–1.
2. He has learned the sounds of the initial consonants as heard in the italicized words.
3. He has not met or learned any of the other 34 words in Table 5–1.
4. By using his knowledge, plus some guidance from the teacher, he should be able to sound out all the words in Table 5–1.

TABLE 5–1   *Identifying Words Using Mental Substitution*

bat	*can*	*fit*	*had*	*map*	*pet*	*run*	*say*
cat	ban	bit	bad	cap	bet	bun	bay
fat	fan	hit	fad	rap	met	fun	hay
hat	man	pit	mad	sap	set	sun	may
mat	pan	sit	pad				pay
pat	ran		sad				ray
rat							

By using the process of thinking the sound of any known consonant and blending this sound with the phonogram that concludes a known sight word, the child should be able to pronounce the new word.

Other techniques for teaching mental substitution follow.

1. Place a known word on the board. Have the children observe closely as you erase the initial *b* and substitute a different known consonant.

    bat   _____ at   cat

Follow the same procedure, substituting other consonants to make easy words, such as f*at,* h*at,* m*at,* and r*at.*

For convenience in building mental substitution exercises, Table 5–2 provides a series of word families. In each, the words end in a common phonogram (*et, ick, ack, ay, ot, an, ill, im, ug, ad*). Not all the words in the table need to be used in beginning reading, and those beginning with blends should not be used in substitution exercises until the sounds of the blends have been taught.

2. *Teacher:* "Change the first letter and make a naming word for 'something living.' "

    Example:
    dish _____ ish   *fish*

log	___ og	hat	___ at	half	____ alf
coat	____ oat	purse	____ urse	nice	____ ice
box	___ ox	mitten	____ itten	grow	____ row
house	____ ouse	rug	____ ug	pull	____ ull

3. *Teacher:* "On the line following each word, write a new word by changing the first letter to the next letter in the alphabet. Then pronounce the new word and use it in a sentence."

bake	_____	cot	_____	fun	_____
ball	_____	cry	_____	fame	_____
book	_____	candy	_____	fate	_____
but	_____	crop	_____	fold	_____

TABLE 5–2 *Words for Teaching Substitution of Initial Consonant Sounds (Words with initial consonant blends are in parentheses.)*

back	bake	day	cap	bug	bank	cot	Dick
Jack	cake	hay	gap	dug	rank	dot	kick
lack	fake	lay	lap	hug	sank	got	lick
pack	lake	may	map	jug	tank	hot	nick
rack	make	pay	nap	mug	(blank)	lot	pick
sack	rake	ray	rap	rug	(crank)	not	sick
tack	sake	say	tap	tug	(drank)	pot	(brick)
(black)	take	way	(clap)	(drug)	(flank)	(blot)	(click)
(crack)	wake	(clay)	(flap)	(plug)	(frank)	(plot)	(slick)
(slack)	(brake)	(play)	(slap)	(slug)	(plank)	(shot)	(stick)
(stack)	(flake)	(stay)	(snap)	(smug)	(prank)	(spot)	(thick)
(track)	(snake)	(tray)	(trap)	(snug)	(spank)	(trot)	(trick)
bag	bail	gain	bat	bump	can	came	Bill
gag	fail	lain	cat	dump	Dan	dame	fill
lag	hail	main	fat	hump	fan	fame	hill
nag	mail	pain	hat	jump	man	game	kill
rag	nail	rain	mat	lump	pan	lame	mill
sag	pail	vain	pat	pump	ran	name	pill
tag	rail	(brain)	rat	(plump)	tan	same	will
wag	sail	(drain)	sat	(slump)	van	tame	(drill)
(brag)	tail	(grain)	(brat)	(stump)	(bran)	(blame)	(skill)
(drag)	(frail)	(plain)	(flat)	(trump)	(clan)	(flame)	(spill)
(flag)	(trail)	(train)	(scat)		(plan)	(frame)	(still)
(snag)	(snail)						
best	bet	bunk	bell	bit	dim	dear	bad
lest	get	dunk	fell	fit	him	fear	dad
nest	jet	hunk	sell	hit	Jim	hear	fad
pest	let	junk	tell	pit	rim	near	had
rest	met	sunk	well	sit	Tim	rear	lad
test	net	(drunk)	yell	wit	(brim)	tear	mad
vest	pet	(flunk)	(smell)	(flit)	(grim)	year	pad
zest	set	(skunk)	(spell)	(grit)	(slim)	(clear)	sad
(blest)	wet	(spunk)	(swell)	(slit)	(swim)	(smear)	(glad)
(crest)	(fret)	(trunk)		(split)	(trim)	(spear)	

gold	_____	lad	_____	met	_____
got	_____	lake	_____	moon	_____
gate	_____	let	_____	mine	_____
gum	_____	line	_____	meat	_____
		lap	_____	mice	_____

Difficulty level can be increased by mixing the words instead of presenting a series of four words.

boat	_____	map	_____	sail	_____
cash	_____	run	_____	rat	_____
fang	_____	sight	_____	bold	_____
ray	_____	bat	_____	sack	_____
kit	_____	kick	_____	ring	_____
lay	_____	vest	_____	kid	_____

Context Plus Minimal Phonic Cue

The following exercise illustrates that, in many situations, the context plus the phonic cue provided by the initial letter of an unknown word will provide enough clues to solve the unknown word. The blank space in each sentence under A could be replaced with several different words. The same blank space in the corresponding sentence under B provides the initial consonant letter of the word. Have children note that when they heed this phonic cue, they can eliminate many of the previously acceptable choices.

Directions: Read the sentences under A. Have children provide a number of words that could fit in each blank. Then read the sentences under B and have the children note their general agreement on choices.

A

1. The _____ would not start.
2. "She is my _____ ," said Billy.
3. Billy asked, "How much _____ do we have?"
4. Which _____ of the year is your favorite?
5. What word _____ in the blank space?

B

1. The c_____ would not start.
2. "She is my s_____ ," said Billy.
3. Billy asked, "How much m_____ do we have?"
4. Which t_____ of the year is your favorite?
5. What word f_____ in the blank space?

Oral Exercise

Directions: Have a volunteer read one of the following incomplete sentences, adding any word that will logically conclude the sentence. Other students then volunteer other words that fit. Stress that no word can fit unless it begins with the sound represented by the letter shown.

Written Exercise

Directions: Children write one (or more) words that begin with the letter shown.

1. Can you see the p_____ ?
2. Is this your b_____ ?
3. This is a t_____ .
4. Here is the c_____ .
5. The girls felt very s_____ .

CONTEXT CLUES AND PHONIC SKILLS: WORKING TOGETHER

Under less than optimal teaching practices, phonics instruction can be so far removed from reading that it inhibits learning to read. All phonics instruction, however, need not focus exclusively on letter-sound relationships. Reading instruction can be made more effective if the learning task involves both reading (context) and a phonics task whose completion depends on the reading task.

In this chapter, as well as in following chapters, phonics instruction is embedded in a "Fun with Language" approach. The learner is asked to read in order to discover what phonics task he is being asked to perform. The difficulty levels of these exercises range from one-word clues to phrases and sentences. These materials can be adapted to almost any phonic teaching: initial, medial, and final consonants; blends, digraphs, and vowel patterns. In all of these exercises, the teacher reads the directions and any sample items with the student.

USING CONTEXT

Teacher: "Read the clue. What do they do? Write the correct word in the space."

Clue			Clue		
dogs	_____	(bark, dark)	cows	_____	(moo, boo)
birds	_____	(sly, fly)	bells	_____	(wing, ring)
boats	_____	(hail, sail)	fires	_____	(turn, burn)
horses	_____	(run, fun)	kings	_____	(mule, rule)
towels	_____	(cry, dry)	frogs	_____	(hop, mop)

Teacher: "Read the clue. Complete the word that fits the clue. Use either *c* or *t* to make a word that fits the clue."

Example:

pretty   _____ ute   use *c* to spell *cute*

story   _____ ale   use *t* to spell *tale*

	Clue			Clue	
1.	money	_____ ash	**6.**	speaking	_____ alk
2.	bath	_____ ub	**7.**	knives	_____ ut
3.	brush	_____ eeth	**8.**	Christmas	_____ ard
4.	bird	_____ age	**9.**	gentle	_____ ame
5.	spins	_____ op	**10.**	penny	_____ ent

Teacher: "Write either *p* or *n* in each blank space to make a word that fits the clue."

	Clue			Clue	
1.	fruit	_____ ear	**6.**	loud	_____ oise
2.	bird	_____ est	**7.**	medicine	_____ ill
3.	fence	_____ ost	**8.**	pecan kernel	_____ ut
4.	two	_____ air	**9.**	sharp	_____ eedle
5.	close	_____ ear	**10.**	writes	_____ en

Teacher: "Read the clue. Add the first letter to make a word that fits the clue."

Example:
you can read it _____ook (b)

	Clue			Clue	
1.	not small	_____ ig	**6.**	season before winter	_____ all
2.	lives on a farm	_____ ig	**7.**	not short	_____ all
3.	false hair	_____ ig	**8.**	round and bounces	_____ all
4.	a dance step	_____ ig	**9.**	from floor to ceiling	_____ all
5.	make a hole in the ground	_____ ig	**10.**	shopping center	_____ all

Teacher: "Write the letter that spells the word that fits the clue. Use *p, b,* or *d.*"

	Clue			Clue	
1.	we read it	_____ ook	**6.**	goes around waist	_____ elt
2.	please open the	_____ oor	**7.**	we sleep on it	_____ ed
3.	lives on a farm	_____ ig	**8.**	worth 10 cents	_____ ime
4.	goes on the water	_____ oat	**9.**	place where we play	_____ ark
5.	a dog is a	_____ et	**10.**	at night it is	_____ ark

Teacher: "Change the first letter in each italicized word so that the new word names something living."

Examples:

I can change *big* to _____ ig. (*pig*)

I can change *see* to _____ ee. (*bee*)

I can change: *hat* to _____ at

dish to _____ ish

pen to _____ en

toy to _____ oy

If a child or group has difficulty with a particular consonant letter sound, develop exercises that focus on this letter. The exercise that follows illustrates *c* and *f*.

Teacher: "Read the clue. Write the letter that spells the word that fits the clue."

Set 1		*Set 2*	
Clue		*Clue*	
1. wear on head	____ ap	**1.** not slow	____ ast
2. catches mice	____ at	**2.** lives in water	____ ish
3. not hot	____ old	**3.** more than four	____ ive
4. grows on farm	____ orn	**4.** after summer	____ all
5. baby cow	____ alf	**5.** less than five	____ our
6. ice cream	____ one	**6.** good to eat	____ ood
7. a baby bear	____ ub	**7.** a tree	____ ir

FUN WITH LANGUAGE

1. Fun with D, F, S, and G Words

Teacher: "Read the clues. Be careful; they're tricky. Complete the word that fits the clue. Use one of the consonant letters *d, f, s,* or *g* to spell the word that fits the clue."

Example:

Clue

not much money	____ ime	*D* is the only letter that fits the clue; a dime is not much money.
front of head	____ ace	Choose *f;* it makes sense.
four legs and butts	____ oat	*G* makes goat, which has four legs. Have you ever heard of a goat butting someone?

	Clue			*Clue*
1. not back, not front	_____ ide	**6.** Don't _____ the bears.	___eed
2. 1492 .... 1776 1976	_____ ates	**7.** always number one	___ irst
3. hole-in-one	_____ olf	**8.** not here now	___ one
4. damp minus *p*	_____ am	**9.** what I owe you	___ ebt
5. goes in shoes	_____ eet	**10.** like the others	___ame

2. The 3-C Sentences!

In the sentences below:

A. Candy is a girl's name. (Candy starts with a capital letter!)
B. She has a candy cane.
C. The three c's get all mixed up, but when you read for meaning it's easy.

Teacher: "Fill in each blank space with one of these words: *Candy, candy,* or *cane.*"

Problem: _____ has a _____ _____ .

Solved: Candy has a candy cane.

1. Does _____ have a _____ _____ ?
2. Yes, the _____ _____ belongs to _____ .
3. Will _____ eat her _____ _____ ?
4. _____ may eat the _____ _____ .
5. Then _____ will not have a _____ _____ .
6. This ends the story of _____ and her _____ _____ .

3. B(ware)—B(ready)—B(sharp)

Teacher: "Every blank space in the following sentences can be filled with the following *b* words: *book, boy,* or *bus.* As you read each sentence write the correct word in each blank space."

1. The _____ has a _____ .
2. The _____ took the _____ on a _____ .
3. The _____ left the _____ on the _____ .
4. The _____ driver found the _____ .
5. He gave the _____ to the _____ .
6. Now the _____ has the _____ .
7. Will the _____ read the _____ ?
8. The _____ read the _____ , but not on the _____!

4. Double D Words

Teacher: "The word *dog* will fit in one space in each sentence below. One other word that also begins with *d* will fit in each of the other spaces. Complete the sentences."

1. _____ the _____ with the towel.
2. The towel will _____ the _____ .
3. The _____ can _____ off in the sun.
4. Will the sun _____ the _____ ?
5. Keep the _____ _____ in winter.

5. **More Double D Words**

   Teacher: "The word *dog* will fit in one blank space in each sentence below. Fill the other space with a word that begins with *d.*"

   Example:

   _____ said, "Where is the _____ ?"
       (Dad)   said, "Where is the   (dog)   ?"

   1. The d_____ sat by the d_____ .
   2. The artist said, "I will d_____ a d_____ .
   3. The d_____ will d_____ the water.
   4. D_____ the d_____ d_____ a hole in the yard?
   5. Yes, the d_____ d_____ d_____ a hole in the yard!

   Teacher: "Need a little help? These words fit the spaces: *dog, did, dig, drink, draw,* and *door.*"

6. **Fun with Triple D Words**

   Teacher: "Each sentence has three missing words. Each missing word begins with the letter *d.* The words *dig, did,* and *dad* fit in each sentence. Where does each word fit?"

   Example:

   D _____ d_____ d_____ this hole?
     (Did)   (dad)   (dig)   this hole?

   1. D_____said he d_____ d_____ that hole.
   2. D_____ d_____ d_____ the hole.
   3. When d_____ d_____ d_____ that hole?
   4. D_____ d_____ not d_____ the hole today.

INITIAL CONSONANT BLENDS

Consonant blends consist of two or more letters that are blended when pronouncing a word. If a child attempts to sound separately each of the consonants in a blend, distortion and confusion will result. These sounds must be blended to arrive at the correct pronunciation. Children already know these speech sounds; they must learn to recognize their printed equivalents. For example, students know the sound of /s/, as heard in *see, sit, some,* and *say,* and the sound of /t/, as heard in *tell, to, talk,* and *top.* The next short step, from the known to the unknown, would be teaching the blend sound */st/,* as heard in *stop, still, stand,* and the like.

Two- and three-letter consonant blends may be divided into three major groups on the basis of a common letter:

- Those in which *r* is the concluding letter (Column A)
- Those in which *l* is the concluding letter (Column B)
- Those that begin with the letter *s* (Column C)

A		B		C
br	scr	bl	spl	sc
cr	spr	cl		sk
dr	str	fl		sm
fr	thr	gl		sn
gr		pl		sp
pr		sl		st
tr				sw

The blends are listed alphabetically, but they may be taught in any order. The two-letter blends are easier to learn and occur more frequently in words met in beginning reading than do the three-letter blends; therefore, it is better to teach the two-letter blends first. See Table 5–3 for words that can be used in teaching consonant blends.

There are several ways to teach children how to master these blend sounds. Regardless of what approach you use, the objectives in teaching blends are to have children (a) see the letter combination involved; (b) realize that in every case the letters combine into a blend sound; and (c) discriminate between the blend sound and the sound of individual letters, as for example, in *pay, lay,* and *play.*

Procedures for teaching initial blends closely parallel those for teaching initial consonant sounds. To illustrate, we will look at the steps in teaching the sound represented by *st* in detail. All other consonant blends may be taught in the same manner.

CHALKBOARD ACTIVITIES

Place a few *st* words on the board, such as *stop, still, star, stand,* and *stick.* Direct children's attention to the *st* beginning. As each word is pronounced, ask the students to listen to the */st/* sound in initial position. Then invite the children to give other words that begin with the blended sounds */st/* (*stone, step, stood, stir*).

TABLE 5–3 *Words for Teaching Initial Consonant Blends*

br	*cr*	*dr*	*fr*	*gr*	*pr*	*tr*
brother	cry	dress	friend	grade	pretty	tree
bring	cross	drink	from	great	present	train
brought	crop	draw	front	ground	president	trip
brown	creek	dry	Friday	green	program	truly
brake	crowd	drive	fruit	grandmother	print	trick
bread	cream	drop	fright	grass	produce	truck
bright	crack	dream	free	grandfather	prize	trade
bridge	crawl	drove	fresh	group	promise	trap
break	crib	drum	frog	grew	proud	track
brave	cried	drew	freeze	gray	product	true
brush	crumb	drill	frozen	grain	prepare	trail
branch	crown	drag	friendly	grab	protect	treat
brick	crow	drank	fry	grape	press	trim
broom	crook	drug	frost	grand	price	tramp

bl	*cl*	*fl*	*pl*	*sl*	*sp*	*st*
black	close	flower	play	sleep	spell	start
blue	clean	fly	place	sled	spend	stay
blow	class	floor	please	slid	spot	story
block	clothes	flag	plant	slate	speak	stop
bloom	climb	flew	plan	slip	spent	store
blew	club	flood	plane	slowly	sport	study
blanket	cloth	float	plenty	slave	speed	still
blood	cloud	flat	plain	slow	spoke	state
blackboard	clear	flour	plate	slipper	spirit	stand
blossom	clay	———	pleasant	slept	speech	stick
blind	clothing	*gl*	plow	sleet	spoon	stocking
blame	clock	———	player	sleepy	spear	step
blizzard	climate	glad	plantation	slim	space	star
blaze	clown	glass	playmate	slick	spin	stood
		glove				

sc	*sk*	*sm*	*sn*	*sw*	*tw*
school	skate	small	snow	swim	twelve
scare	skin	smoke	snake	sweet	twist
scold	sky	smell	snowball	swing	twenty
scout	ski	smile	snail	sweater	twice
scream	skip	smart	snap	swan	twin
schoolhouse	skirt	smooth	snug	sweep	twig
score	skunk	smack	sneeze	swell	twinkle

AUDITORY-VISUAL ASSOCIATION

1. Key Words (Two-letter Blends)

   a. Duplicate a series of key words that emphasize the common letter in a number of consonant blends, such as *r*, *l*, and *s*. Provide each child with a copy.
   b. Lead children in seeing and saying the blends and the key words in each column: /br/ as in *bring,* /cr/ as in *cry,* /dr/ as in *drum.*

See the *r*		See the *l*		Begins with *s*	
br	*bring*	bl	*blue*	sc	*school*
cr	*cry*	cl	*clean*	sk	*sky*
dr	*drum*	fl	*fly*	sm	*small*
fr	*from*	gl	*glad*	sn	*snow*
gr	*green*	pl	*play*	sp	*spot*
pr	*pretty*	sl	*slow*	st	*stop*
tr	*tree*			sw	*swim*

2. Hearing Blends in Words (Identifying Blends Heard)

   a. Prepare columns showing three different blends.
   b. Pronounce a word that begins with one of the blends shown: *"blue," "stand," "train,"* and so on.
   c. Children underline the blend that is heard at the beginning of the stimulus word.

blue	*stand*	*train*	*play*	*smoke*
br	st	gl	pr	sn
pl	sl	tr	bl	sm
bl	sm	sk	pl	sp

3. Word Recognition (Auditory-to-Visual Patterns)

   a. Duplicate a number of three-word series as shown.
   b. Pronounce one word from each series. (The stimulus word is italicized here, but would not be on hand-out material supplied to children.)
   c. Children underline the word pronounced.

1	*2*	*3*	*4*	*5*
black	stay	smell	skin	*flew*
back	gay	*spell*	*sing*	few
brick	*gray*	sell	swing	true

6	*7*	*8*	*9*	*10*
snail	sin	dumb	grain	bake
scale	sink	*drum*	*rain*	*brake*
sail	*skin*	from	gain	rake

PRINT AND SOUND

1. Add a Blend

Here the student writes the two letters that represent the initial blended sounds.

Teacher: "Write the letters that are shown above the blank spaces. Then pronounce the words you have made."

br	*sp*	*cl*	*sw*
_____ain	_____eak	_____ean	_____im
_____ake	_____oon	_____oth	_____eet
_____an	_____ace	_____ay	_____ay
_____own	_____in	_____imb	_____ell
_____ush	_____ell	_____ock	_____ing

2. Change a Blend

Use word endings that will make different words when different blends are added.

Teacher: "In each blank space write the blend shown on the left. Then pronounce each word."

(br) _____own	(sp) _____ill	(sk) _____ate
(cr) _____own	(st) _____ill	(pl) _____ate
(dr) _____own	(sk) _____ill	(st) _____ate
(fr) _____own	(dr) _____ill	(cr) _____ate
	(gr) _____ill	(sl) _____ate

 USING CONTEXT

Teacher: "Read the clue. Write a two-letter blend to make a word that goes with the clue."

Examples:

snake _____awls
(a snake *cr*awls, so use *cr*)

fruit _____ and
(you can buy fruit at the fruit *st*and)

Note: All tasks in Set 1 begin with the same blend found in the clue. In Set 2 they are all different.

	Set 1		*Set 2*
Clue		*Clue*	
fresh	_____uit	snow	_____ake
tree	_____unk	broom	_____eeps
train	_____ack	scare	_____ow
brown	_____ead	draw	_____idge
sleds	_____ide	glue	_____icks
travel	_____ip	tree	_____ump

Teacher: "Read the clue. Complete the word that fits the clue. Use one of the blends *st, sp,* or *sn* to make a word that fits the clue."

Examples:

a place to buy	_____ore	use *st* to spell *store*
football, tennis	_____orts	use *sp* to spell *sports*

Clue		*Clue*	
1. hard metal	_____eel	**6.** to say something	_____eak
2. slow as a	_____ail	**7.** shines at night	_____ar
3. tops do this	_____in	**8.** sleep noise	_____ore
4. eat with this	_____oon	**9.** bees can	_____ing
5. to begin	_____art	**10.** as white as	_____ow

Teacher: "Write one of the blends *sl, sw,* or *sk* in the blank spaces to make a word that fits the clue."

Clue		*Clue*	
1. using a broom	_____eep	**6.** above the earth	_____y
2. women wear	_____irts	**7.** moves on snow	_____ed
3. not fast	_____ow	**8.** a beautiful fowl	_____an
4. very clever	_____y	**9.** arm goes in	_____eeve
5. a bunch of bees	_____arm	**10.** smells bad	_____unk

Teacher: "Write the blend that spells the word that fits the clue."

Examples:

pleased and happy _____ad (gl)   train runs on it _____ack (tr)

Clue Box				
sl	tr	bl	cl	sp

1. near by   _____ose

2. close your eyes and   _____eep

3. what a top does   _____in

4. cannot see   _____ind

5. used to catch lobsters _____ap

6. to go up the hill   _____imb

7. runs on track   _____ain

8. to say something   _____eak

9. a pretty color   _____ue

10. not very fast   _____ow

Teacher: "Read the clue. Write the word that fits the clue."

Example:

can write on this _____ (skate, *slate*)

    Clue

1. food is placed on this   _____   (state, plate)

2. not big or large   _____   (small, star)

3. this jumps in the pond   _____   (frog, drop)

4. not very far away   _____   (slow, close)

5. what we do with a broom _____   (sweep, speak)

Teacher: "How many *s*tudents can *s*tand on a *s*tump? Each of the following sentences has two missing words. The words *stand* and *stump* will fit in each sentence. Where does each word fit?"

Example:

Can you _____ on a _____ ?

Teacher: "This is easy; the context forces you to write: Can you *stand* on a *stump?* Finish the following sentences."

1. You can _____ on a _____ .

2. A _____ can _____ in the woods.

3. A _____ can _____ a long time.

4. We can both _____ on this large _____ .

5. Can this _____ _____ for 50 years?

Teacher: "Since you are well *g*rounded in reading, it will be easy to *p*low through this exercise. Just *p*lant a few words in the blank spaces. Each sentence has two missing words. Two of the words *plow, plant,* or *ground* will fit in each sentence. Which two words fit where?"

Example:

After you _____ you can _____ crops.

Teacher: "When you use the context of the sentence, you will probably make it read: After you *plow,* you can *plant* crops. Complete each of the following sentences using *plow, plant,* or *ground.*"

1. You must _____ the _____ in the spring.

2. Then you _____ seeds in the _____ .

3. You must _____ before you _____ .

4. Remember, _____ seeds after you _____ .

5. Always prepare the _____ before you _____ .

Teacher: "One of the letter clusters in the clue box will complete *all* the words in one sentence. Study each sentence and fill in the blanks."

Clue Box				
gr	cl	tr	st	dr

Example:

They _____ew many kinds of _____ ain on the farm. (gr)

1. The _____ own will _____ ean the _____ othes.

2. He _____ ood ready to _____art telling the _____ ory.

3. She did not _____ op the _____ um during the _____ ill.

4. It was a _____ eat to _____amp along the _____ail.

5. She _____ove to town to buy a _____ess.

Teacher: "John makes many speeches. The sentences that follow are all about John and his speeches. All blanks in these sentences are filled by one of these words:

   sp*eak*   sp*oke*   sp*oken*   sp*eaking*   sp*eaks*   sp*eaker*

—Wait! The last word in the last sentence begins with a different blend."

1. John was invited to sp_____ .

2. He is sp_____ now.

3. He will sp_____ again tomorrow.

4. He sp_____ twice this week.

5. He has sp_____many times this year.

6. He is a very good sp_____ .

7. After he sp_____ he will eat a _____eak!

INITIAL CONSONANT DIGRAPHS
(*SH, WH, TH,* AND *CH*)

A digraph is a combination of two letters that represent one speech sound. The sound heard is not a blend of the two letters involved, but a completely new sound. A given digraph may have more than one pronunciation, but the letter combination results in a single sound in each case (*ch* = /k/ in *chorus;* /sh/ in *chef;* /ch/ in *church*). Digraphs may be taught in a similar way to that used for teaching consonant sounds.

Steps in Brief

1. Place several stimulus words on the chalkboard: *shall, she, ship,* and *show.*
2. Ask the children to look at the words carefully and note how they are alike. Draw out the observation that all the words begin with *sh.* (Underline the digraph being taught: *sh, ch, th,* or *wh.*)
3. Ask the children to listen to the sound of /sh/ as they say the words together.
4. Invite children to supply other words that begin with the same sound as *shall, she, ship,* and *show.*

Note: The digraph *sh* usually has the sound heard in these stimulus words. Other common *sh* words are *shut, shop, shot, sheep, shape, shade, short, sheet, shoot, shoe, shell, shirt, shovel, shake, sharp,* and *shine.*

The digraph *wh* is usually pronounced as if spelled *hw:* when = hwen; white = hwite. The /wh/ sound may be taught as /sh/ was above, with *when, white, what,* and *which* as stimulus words. Other common *wh* words are *why, where, wheel, wheat, whisper, whether, whale,* and *whiskers.* Exceptions: When *o* follows *wh,* the *w* is silent, as in who = h$\overline{oo}$; whole = hōl; whom = h$\overline{oo}$m; whose = h$\overline{oo}$z. (Changing patterns of pronunciation have likely caused some dictionaries to recognize a second pronunciation: when = wĕn.)

The digraph *th* has two common sounds. There is the voiced /th/ sound as in *this, their, they, though, that, then, there, than,* and *them,* and the unvoiced *th* sound as in *thing, thin, thimble, thank, think, thick, third,* and *thumb.* (The concepts of voiced and unvoiced need not be taught in relation to reading.)

While the consonant digraph *ch* has three different sounds, the most common and the one met almost exclusively in beginning reading is that of /ch/ heard in *chair* or *chop.* Common words for use in teaching *ch* exercises include the following.

chair	chin	chose	charm	chalk
child	check	chop	chance	cheer
chicken	cheek	change	chimney	chief

Much later, children will meet the other sounds represented by *ch*. These need not be taught in beginning reading.

ch = k		*ch = sh*	
chorus	(kō rus)	chef	(shef)
character	(kar ak ter)	chassis	(shas ē)
chemist	(kem ist)	chauffeur	(sho fur)
choir	(kwir)	chic	(shēk)
chord	(kord)	chiffon	(shif on)
chrome	(krom)	chamois	(sham ē)

Blends in Sentence Context

Prepare a number of sentences in which a high percentage of the words begin with the digraphs *sh, ch, wh,* and *th*. These may be presented via the chalkboard, transparencies, or duplicated worksheets. After reading the material silently, children volunteer to read a sentence to the group.

1. Charles and Chip chatted in the church chapel.
2. Chester chose a chunk of cheese and some chips from the chest.
3. Shirley showed the shells to Sherman.
4. The shepherd sheltered the sheep in the shadow of the shed.
5. His white whiskers were whirled by the whistling wind.
6. Mr. White whispered when and where the whale would appear.
7. On Thursday, Thelma thought of thirty things to do.
8. Thad thought about a thorn in his thumb.

USING CONTEXT

Teacher: "Read the clue word. Following each clue, complete a word that has the opposite meaning. Use one of the digraphs *ch, th, sh,* or *wh* to do this."

Example:

pride _____ame (write *sh* for *shame*)

	Clue				*Clue*	
1.	adult	_____ild		**3.**	open	_____ut
2.	tall	_____ort		**4.**	fat	_____in

5. shout	_____isper	**8.** freeze	_____aw
6. dull	_____arp	**9.** thin	_____ick
7. retreat	_____arge	**10.** warm	_____illy

Teacher: "Read the clue. Build a word, using *ch, sh, th,* or *wh,* that fits the clue."

Example:

can dig with this _____ovel (sh)

Clue

1. fits on foot	_____oe
2. not very tall	_____ort
3. round and rolls	_____eel
4. speaking very softly	_____isper
5. writes on blackboard	_____alk
6. leader of the tribe	_____ief
7. one on each hand	_____umb
8. after first and second	_____ird
9. we sit on this	_____air
10. found on the beach	_____ell

Teacher: "Each sentence shows two words containing blank spaces. One digraph—*ch, sh, th,* or *wh*—will fit the blanks in both words. Study each sentence and complete each word."

Example:

Don't let the (*ch*)icken eat the (*ch*)alk.

1. The _____eep were resting in the _____ade.
2. Who put the _____alk mark on the _____air?
3. _____ich of the _____eels is broken?
4. He bought a _____irt in the _____op.
5. She had a _____imble on her _____umb.
6. After a purchase, always _____eck your _____ange.

⌒   FUN WITH LANGUAGE

Teacher: "Each sentence below contains some incomplete words. A digraph—*ch, th, sh,* or *wh*—is missing in each word. Read the clue box carefully and then complete the sentences."

> **Clue Box**
> Chuck and Sue plan to go shopping.
> Knowing this will help you.
> Remember, the missing parts are *ch, th, sh,* or *wh.*

1. Sue said, "_____ere _____all we _____op?"
2. _____uck said, "And _____at _____all we buy?"
3. I _____ink we _____ould _____eck the ads," said _____uck.
4. _____en I will _____op for _____oes and a _____irt.
5. Sue wanted to _____op for _____ite _____oes.
6. I _____ink _____ey _____ould have fun _____ile _____opping!

THE *WH* ROUNDUP

Teacher: Tease out the meaning. In the following sentences, each unfinished word begins with *wh. Wh*ich word goes *wh*ere? All sentences are based on the clue box.

> **Clue Box**
> "Sam lives in a white house on Whale Street."

Finish each word so that it makes sense in the sentence.

1. Wh_____ house on Wh_____ Street is Sam's house?
2. Sam lives on Wh_____ Street in a wh_____ house.
3. Sam, wh_____ house is wh_____ , lives on Wh_____ Street.
4. Wh_____ house is the wh_____ house wh_____ Sam lives?
5. Wh_____ on Wh_____ Street is Sam's wh_____ house?
6. Wh_____ did Sam move into the wh_____ house?

FINAL CONSONANTS, BLENDS, AND DIGRAPHS

Some of the procedures for teaching initial sounds can be adapted to teaching final sounds. The teaching objective remains the same: to help children visually recognize letter forms and associate these with the sounds they represent in words.

1. Chalkboard Drill
a. Select the letter-sound to be taught.
b. Place stimulus words on the board.
c. Call children's attention to the final letter.
d. Pronounce each word carefully, so that children hear the sound at the end of the word.
e. Have children pronounce words and supply others that end with the sound.

2. Print and Sound
a. Prepare columns of easy words, all of which end with a particular letter-sound.
b. Omit the final letter.
c. Children print the letter indicated and pronounce the word.

Add d	Add n	Add p	Add g	Add t
sa____	gu____	li____	ho____	ne____
mu____	wi____	ca____	pi____	hu____
ha____	te____	na____	ta____	co____
ro____	ru____	cu____	wi____	hi____

Variations:
Add *m, x,* or *b* to make a word. Pronounce each word.

bo____	gu____	ro____	dru____	fo____
roo____	mi____	ha____	gra____	so____
hi____	tu____	si____	wa____	ta____

Change the last letter of words in the first column so that the new word names something living.

Example:

pin	pi____	(g)	pig
plane	plan____	(t)	plant

1. but	bu____		**6.** map	ma____
2. lamp	lam____		**7.** dot	do____
3. fog	fo____		**8.** hem	he____
4. call	cal____		**9.** owe	ow____
5. cap	ca____		**10.** sharp	shar____

USING CONTEXT

Teacher: "Finish each of the following sentences so that it makes sense. Put the letter *m* or *n* in each blank space. You must read carefully to know which letter fits into which blank."

Example:

Pa____ had a talk with a ma____ .

Teacher: "'Pan had a talk with a mam' makes no sense. The sentence 'Pam had a talk with a man' is correct. Remember that every blank has to be filled with *m* or *n*."

1. Sa____ can count to te____ .
2. Ca____ you see the me____ ?
3. She gave hi____ a stick of gu____ .
4. Please pass the ha____ .
5. Mo____ put ja____ on the bu____ .

The purpose of the following exercise is to provide practice in hearing the letter sounds *p, d,* and *b* at the end of words.

Teacher: "Finish each sentence below so that it makes sense. Put *b, d,* or *p* in each blank space. You must read carefully to know which letter fits in each space."

Example:

A baby bear is a cu____ . (can't be cup or cud)

A baby bear is a cub.

Set 1

1. Turn on the lam____ .
2. They rode in a taxi ca____ .
3. He took a short na____ .
4. I like corn on the co____ .
5. A bee stung him on the han____ .

Set 2

1. Bo_____ plays in the ban_____ .
2. The guide said, "Here is the ma_____ ."
3. The water in the tu_____ was col_____ .
4. Di_____ he leave his ca_____ in the ca_____ ?
5. Mother said, "Gra_____ the pu_____ ."

The following are some stimulus words to use in board or seatwork exercises:

b	*d*	*f*	*g*	*k (ck)*	*l (ll)*	*m*
Bob	sad	if	dog	back	call	him
tub	fed	calf	big	rock	tell	room
club	send	muff	flag	black	hill	gum
grab	glad	stiff	rug	trick	pull	ham
rob	cold	puff	drug	duck	still	whom
rib	band	off	bag	pick	small	drum

n	*p*	*r*	*s (s)*	*s (=z)*	*t*
can	hop	for	bus	his	cat
win	cap	star	yes	as	met
men	stop	her	dress	ours	shut
thin	up	dear	us	is	hit
when	step	door	less	has	set
ran	skip	clear	likes	runs	sat
moon	map	car	miss	days	but

Consonant Digraphs *ch, sh,* and *th* at the End of Words

The sounds of the digraphs *ch, sh,* and *th* will have been taught already because they occur at the beginning of words. Procedures for teaching these sounds at the end of words may parallel those used for teaching initial sounds.

1. Place stimulus words on the board.
2. Have the children look at the letter combinations under discussion.
3. Pronounce each word carefully so children hear the sound at the end of the word.
4. Have the children pronounce the words.

```
Which

reach

such

pitch
```

Other stimulus words ending with *ch, sh,* or *th* are *March, church, peach, branch, ditch, search, teach, patch, bench; fish, cash, fresh, rush, crash, dish, flash, wish, push; both, bath, tenth, north, health, path, length, fifth,* and *cloth.*

USING CONTEXT

Teacher: "Read the clue word. Complete the word that follows, using one of the digraphs *ch, sh,* or *th.*"

Clue Word		Clue Word	
fruit	pea_____	vegetable	squa_____
two	bo_____	direction	nor_____
month	Mar_____	meal	lun_____
money	ca_____	insect	mo_____
lightning	fla_____	wreck	cra_____
trail	pa_____	worship	chur_____

Teacher: "Some language games are easier than they look! To complete the following sentences you must write one of the digraphs *ch, sh,* or *th* in each blank space. Reading the rest of the sentence makes it easy."

Example:

Eat fre_____ fi_____ for your heal_____ .

Teacher: "The only way for the sentence to make sense is by using *ch, sh,* or *th* in the three blanks. Remember, either *ch, sh,* or *th* will fit in each blank."

1. "Are the fi_____ fre_____ ?" he asked.
2. Bo_____ nor_____ and sou_____ are directions.
3. A bran_____ fell from the pea_____ tree.
4. The parade will mar_____ down the pa_____ .
5. Whi_____ clo_____ needs the pat_____ ?
6. We had fre_____ fi_____ for lun_____ .
7. Mar_____ is the third mon_____ .

Consonant Digraphs *nk, ng,* and *ck* at the End of Words

Teaching *nk, ng,* and *ck* involves associating these letter combinations at the end of words or syllables with the sounds they represent. These digraphs may be taught by instructing children that, for example, "The sound of /nk/ at the end of words is the sound we hear in these words."

bank	link	junk
rank	mink	sunk
sank	pink	drunk
tank	sink	shrunk

Other words to use in board or seatwork exercises include *ink, blink, drink, think; plank, drank, spank, frank; trunk, chunk,* and *bunk.*

"The sound of /ng/ at the end of words is the sound we hear in these words."

bang	king	gong	hung
gang	ring	bong	rung
hang	wing	strong	sprung
sang	sing	song	sung

"The letters *ck* have the sound of /k/. Listen to the sound at the end of these words."

back	pick	dock	luck
pack	kick	lock	duck
sack	sick	block	truck
crack	trick	sock	buck

Final Consonant Blends (*st, sk, ld, mp,* and *nd*)

Teaching procedures described throughout this chapter can be used or adapted to teach blended consonants occurring at the end of words (*st, sk, ld, mp,* and *nd*).

must	ask	cold	jump	find
fast	desk	wild	camp	band
rest	mask	field	dump	found
most	dusk	child	champ	bend

CONSONANT IRREGULARITIES

Fortunately, sounds represented by consonant letters involve less variability than is found in vowel letter-sounds. Nevertheless, a number of consonants and consonant combinations result in pronunciation irregularities that must be taught. The majority of these fall into one of the following groupings.

- Consonants that have more than one sound (for example, *c* sounded as /k/ or /s/; *g* sounded as /g/ or /j/; and *s* sounded as /s/, /z/, /sh/, or /zh/)

- Consonants that are not sounded (know, light, wrap)
- Consonant combinations with unique pronunciations (*ph* = /f/; *que* = /k/)

The Two Sounds of *c* (/k/ and /s/)

The letter *c* represents no distinctive sound of its own. It is sounded as /k/ when followed by the vowels *a, o,* and *u,* and as /s/ when followed by *i, e,* or *y.* The hard (k) sound occurs most frequently and for this reason is usually taught first. Eight words on the Dolch List begin with the letter *c,* and in all of these the letter has its /k/ sound. Only four of the 58 words on the Dale List that begin with *c* have the /s/ sound. Chalkboard and duplicated seatwork exercises can provide drill as needed. Here are some examples.

c is sounded /k/ when followed by	a	o	u
	call	cold	cut
	cake	come	cup
	care	coat	cute
	cap	cook	cub
c is sounded /s/ when followed by	i	e	y
	city	cent	cymbal
	cinder	cement	cypress
	cider	mice	cynic
	citizen	voice	cylinder

Some words include both sounds of c: *circle, cycle,* and *circus.*
Teacher: "Say each word softly aloud, then on each blank space write *s* or *k* to show the sound of the letter *c.*"

_____cat	_____comb	_____ceiling	_____color
_____center	_____citizen	_____cuff	_____cellar

The Two Sounds of *g* (/g/ and /j/)

1. The letter *g* has its regular (hard) sound when followed by *a, u,* and *o.*
2. The letter *g* is often sounded as /j/ when followed by *i, e,* and *y.* (Common exceptions: *give, girl, get, geese,* and *gift.*)

Dealing with the two sounds of *g* is not so much a matter of teaching but of simply acquainting children with this phenomenon. Only a few words are met in beginning reading in which *g* is sounded as /j/. After stating the two rules, children may practice hearing the two sounds.

Teacher: "Pronounce each word softly, then on each blank space write *g* or *j* to show the sound that *g* represents."

_____George	_____goat	_____gem	_____game
_____gum	_____giant	_____gave	_____gentle
_____garden	_____general	_____gold	_____gun

Sounds Represented by the Letter *s*

1. The letter *s* usually represents its regular sound as heard in *said, set, sing, soap,* and *sun.*
2. The letter *s* is sometimes sounded as /z/ when it is the final sound in the word: *is, his, has, ours, please, cheese,* and *noise.*
3. The letter *s* is sounded /sh/ in *sure* and *sugar.*
4. The letter *s* is sounded /zh/ in *measure* and *treasure.*

It is highly doubtful that the irregularities associated with the letter *s* have any significant impact on learning to read.

Consonants Not Sounded

A large number of English words contain one or more letters that are not sounded. In some instances, particularly when the initial letter is not sounded, it pays to learn the words as sight words. Instant word recognition and independent reading are enhanced by deliberately calling to children's attention the more frequently occurring instances of consonants that are not sounded. We can make the following generalizations.

1. In words containing double consonants, the first is sounded, the second is not.
2. In words beginning with *kn,* the *k* is usually not sounded.
3. The combination *gh* is usually not sounded when preceded by the vowel *i.*
4. In words beginning with *wr,* the *w* is usually not sounded.
5. In words ending with the syllable *-ten,* the *t* is often not sounded.
6. The digraph *ck* is pronounced *k.*
7. In words ending with *mb,* the *b* is usually not sounded.

It is doubtful that learning these rules in isolation or as a series of generalizations has virtue. Working with a series of stimulus words that follow one or more of the rules will help children gain insight into the pronunciation of words. Table 5–4 provides examples of words that follow each of these seven generalizations.

While a given generalization may be introduced in a particular grade, it will probably have to be reviewed in subsequent grades. For some children, simple review will not be adequate, and the generalization and applications will have to be retaught. By means of close observation or diagnosis, the teacher—at any grade level—discovers which children need help on a particular skill and can work individually with these children or devise seatwork exercises that provide practice in the areas in which deficiencies are noted. Words of appropriate difficulty can be selected for use in various types of teaching exercises. The difficulty level of the exercises can be further controlled by the task or tasks the children are called upon to perform.

TABLE 5–4   *Consonants Not Sounded*

Double Consonants	kn Words	gh Words	wr Words	-ten Ending	-ck Ending	-mb Ending
ladder	know	sigh	write	often	sack	comb
collect	knee	light	wring	soften	neck	thumb
fellow	knight	sight	wrote	listen	block	climb
message	knew	bright	wrap	hasten	kick	bomb
roller	knit	flight	wrath	fasten	duck	lamb
summer	knife	night	wrist	glisten	clock	plumb
dinner	knock	might	wrong	moisten	black	limb
yellow	kneel	slight	wren	brighten	trick	numb
happen	knob	blight	wreck	tighten	back	crumb
kitten	known	right	wreath	frighten	pick	dumb

The purpose of the following exercises is to explain the concept that some letters in words may not represent a sound. At this level, one need not explain in the language of linguistic science. The term *silent letters* is inaccurate, since no letters make sounds; however, to use this term with six-year-olds is not poor pedagogy.

1. *Directions:* Place material on the chalkboard similar to the examples in the box. Pronounce each word. Call attention to the pair of like consonants and the fact that they represent one sound. Draw a slash through the second consonant in each pair to indicate that it is not sounded.

> *summer dress letter bell*
> Two like consonants stand for one sound.
> letter summer dress bell

Put words on the chalkboard that illustrate this concept or duplicate material for seatwork. Have children cross out the letter that is not sounded.

dinner	kitten	tall
glass	cuff	barrel
ball	ladder	yellow
hidden	doll	fuzz
cross	grass	sudden
rabbit	happen	class

2. *Purpose:* To provide practice in sight recognition of words that contain one or more of the irregular spellings *kn, wr, igh, mb, ph* = /f/, and *gh* = /f/.

   Directions: Explain the irregularities of the letter combinations discussed. Have the children note that the words in each line contain the letter pattern shown on the left. Have them practice pronouncing each word and learn these words as sight words.

kn:	knew known knee knight knit knock know
	(the *k* is not sounded)
wr:	write wrong wreck wrote wring wrap wrist
	(the *w* is not sounded)
igh:	light night sight bright right fight might
	(*i* = ī; *gh* is not sounded)
mb:	comb lamb thumb climb crumb bomb
	(the final letter *b* is not sounded)
ph:	phone photo nephew phonics autograph phrase
	(*ph* represents the sound of /f/)
gh:	laugh cough rough enough tough laughter
	(final letters represent the sound of /f/)

3. *Directions:* Have the children read the following sentences softly aloud to themselves, then underline the letters *kn, wr, ph, gh,* and *mb* each time they appear in a word.
   1. The knight knew how to write, so he wrote a pamphlet.
   2. He took a right turn on the wrong light and had a wreck.
   3. The wreck was quite a sight in the bright moonlight.
   4. Phil hurt his knee and thumb taking photographs that night.
   5. If you know the alphabet and phonics, you can learn to read and write.

4. *Teacher:* "Pronounce all the words in each A column. Then strike out each silent consonant in the words in the A columns. The first one is done for you. In the space under B, write the dictionary pronunciation of each word." (This will be used later in conjunction with dictionary work.)

A	*B*	*A*	*B*
sig̸h̸t	sīt	knig̸h̸t	nīt
hasten	___	glisten	___
knew	___	comb	___
rabbit	___	right	___
thick	___	write	___
climb	___	black	___

wrote	_____	funnel	_____
dollar	_____	known	_____
debt	_____	doubt	_____
knock	_____	truck	_____
soften	_____	often	_____
summer	_____	tunnel	_____
sigh	_____	thumb	_____

5. The following exercise illustrates that unsounded letters are useful in that they produce a different word that has the same pronunciation but a different meaning from the word to which the unsounded letter is added. This letter provides a visual clue to the meaning of the new word.

Teacher: "In column B, add a letter that is not sounded to each word in column A in order to produce a different word."

A	B	A	B
new	_____	night	_____
hole	_____	be	_____
our	_____	cent	_____
rap	_____	not	_____
nob	_____	plum	_____
in	_____	ring	_____

Qu and *Que* Combinations (/*kw*/ and /*k*/)

Qu.   The letter *q* has no sound of its own and is always followed by *u*, which in this case does not function as a vowel. The combination *qu* is pronounced /*kw*/, as in *quick = kwik* and *quack = kwak*.

Other *qu* words that might be used in teaching exercises include *queen, quart, quiet, quit, Quaker, quake, quite, quarter, quail,* and *quarrel.*

Que.   *Que* at the end of words has the sound of /*k*/; usually *que* is blended with the preceding syllable.

picturesque = pĭk chûr ĕsk	plaque = plăk
antique = ăn tēk	grotesque = grō tĕsk
burlesque = bûr lĕsk	clique = klēk
opaque = ō pāk	brusque = brŭsk
critique = krĭ tēk	technique = tĕk nēk

Note that the final syllable in *que* words is accented.

SUMMARY

In this chapter, we built on children's previously acquired skills of auditory-visual discrimination and dealt with teaching consonant letter-sound relationships. There is a good rationale for teaching consonants in initial position in words. You now have steps for teaching single letters, blends (clusters), and digraphs, and suggestions for helping children master certain consonant letter-sound irregularities.

In general, consonant letters are quite consistent in the sounds they represent. Letters that represent only one sound include *b, d, h, j, k, l, m, n, p, r, w,* and initial *y.*

Consonants that combine include the following:

- *Consonant blends* (clusters), in which two or more letters blend so that sound elements of each letter are heard: *bl, bl*ack; *str, str*ing; *spl, spl*ash; and *gl, gl*ide.
- *Consonant digraphs,* in which two-letter combinations result in one speech sound that is not a blend of the letters involved: *sh*all; *wh*ite; *th*is (voiced */th/*); *th*ink (unvoiced */th/*); *ch*air; *ch*orus (*ch* = */k/*); and *ch*ef (*ch* = */sh/*).

Some consonants and consonant combinations have irregular spellings.

Unsounded Consonants in Specific Combinations

1. The *k* is not sounded in *kn* (k̶new, k̶nee)
2. Double consonants—only one is sounded (summ̶er)
3. When the vowel *i* precedes *gh,* the latter is not sounded (lig̶h̶t)
4. The *w* is not sounded in *wr* at the beginning of words (w̶riting)
5. When a word ends with the syllable *-ten,* the *t* is often not sounded (oft̶en, fast̶en)
6. The *ck* combination is pronounced */k/* (sac̶k, cloc̶k)
7. The *b* is not sounded in *mb* at the end of words (comb̶, lamb̶)

There are two sounds for the consonant *c.*

1. c = */k/* in *cake, corn,* and *curl*
2. c = */s/* when followed by *i, e,* or *y* (*city, cent, cycle*)

There are two sounds for the consonant *g.*

1. regular sound in *go, game,* and *gum*
2. g = */j/* when followed by *e* or *i* (*gem, giant*)

Other irregularities include the following.

1. *ph* = */f/* (*photo* = *foto; graph* = *graf*)
2. *qu* = */kw/* (*quack* = *kwack*). The letter *q* has no sound of its own. In English spellings, *q* is always followed by the letter *u.*
3. The letter *s* may be sounded in a number of ways.
   a. *s* = */s/* (most common) (*sell, soft, said*)
   b. *s* = */z/* (*his* = *hiz; runs* = *runz*)
   c. *s* = */sh/* (*sugar*)
   d. *s* = */zh/* (*treasure*)

Chapter 6

VOWEL LETTER-SOUND RELATIONSHIPS

*T*eaching the vowel letter-sound relationships is undoubtedly the most difficult and confusing part of an entire phonics program. This stems from two factors:

1. The variability of the sounds that vowels represent.
2. The tendency to overteach certain vowel letter-sound relationships, which can be confusing rather than helpful.

We have discussed the variability of vowel letter-sounds in Chapter 1. In essence, all the rules or generalizations that have been advanced to cover vowel letter-sounds turn out to have numerous exceptions. Nevertheless, to be successful in the decoding process, children must develop insights relative to the relationship between visual letter patterns and the sounds these patterns *usually* represent. The apparent variability in spelling and sounds should point up the fact that a number of high-frequency words should be learned as sight words. A list of these sight words is provided in Table 6–1 at the end of this chapter.

PHONICS INSTRUCTION AS OVERKILL

The second problem in teaching vowel letter-sound relationships stems from the fact that teachers and schools sometimes forget the limited purpose of phonics instruction in the learning-to-read process (see Figure 6–1). Two issues emerge. Do we teach some "phonics" that has relatively little impact on learning to read? Do we overteach some facets of letter-sound relationships that are more appropriate for producing junior linguists rather than beginning readers?

When our goal is simply teaching children to read, some minute differences in letter-sounds need not be dealt with at all. Certain other differences can be pointed

FIGURE 6–1   The cartoonist Malcolm Hancock suggests that phonics can be overtaught as he shows an artistic disdain for vowels

out without forcing children to spend time discriminating these sounds in lists of words. What we sometimes forget in dealing with native speakers of English is that children can pronounce and thus differentiate among words that contain different sound values for a given vowel, such as *a* in *almost, loyal, path, idea,* and *father.* Furthermore, when children are reading for meaning, the problem diminishes in importance.

SEQUENCE IN TEACHING VOWEL LETTER-SOUNDS

There are certain factors relating to the sequence of teaching skills that have served as the basis for lengthy debate. Many of these may be of little importance to children learning to read, which vowel letter-sound to teach first, whether to teach short or long sounds first, or whether to teach these two sounds concomitantly are probably not crucial issues. In fact, a quite reasonable rationale could be made for opposite views pertaining to most matters of sequence.

In advocating the teaching of short vowel sounds first, it can be pointed out that a majority of the words children meet in beginning reading contain short vowel sounds. Many of these words are single-vowel-in-medial-position words. The phonic generalization for this situation—one vowel in medial position usually has its short sound—applies in a large percentage of words met in beginning reading.

Advocacy of teaching long vowel sounds first rests on the fact that the vowel name is the long sound of the vowel (*a, e, i, o, u*). It is frequently suggested that this fact makes it easy to teach the letter-sound association.

SHORT VOWEL SOUNDS

The generalizations that cover short vowel sounds deal primarily with initial single vowels and single vowels in medial position in words. Both of these vowel situations can be covered by the statement, "A single vowel that does not conclude a word usually has its short sound"; for example, *am, an, and, ant, as, ask, at,* and *act.*

The vast majority of words covered have a vowel in medial position, however, and as a result, the following generalization is used more frequently: "A single vowel in medial position usually has its short sound," as we see when we add an initial consonant to the words for the first generalization: *ham, can, hand, pant, gas, task, bat,* and *fact.*

We will illustrate methods for teaching the short vowel sound in medial position. To avoid repetition, we will use a teaching procedure to illustrate only one vowel sound; however, any of the approaches described can be used to teach each of the other vowel letter-sounds that fit the generalization. You will also find brief word lists for teaching each of the vowel letter-sounds.

For the short sound of *a* (ă), explain to children that they have learned a number of the sounds consonants represent in words and that they will now practice hearing one of the sounds represented by the vowel *a.*

> Teacher: "When we say the name of the vowel letter, we hear what is called the vowel's long sound."
>
> "Today we are going to listen carefully and learn to hear another sound for the vowel *a*—its short sound. I am going to put some words on the board. We have studied these words before. Each of the words has the letter *a* in it. Listen to the sound the *a* has in each word."

Begin by writing these words on the chalkboard: *man, had, back, ran, cap, tag.*

1. Pronounce each word, moving your hand from left to right through the word.
2. Emphasize the sound /ă/ in each word, but do not distort the sound.
3. Have the children say the words in unison, asking them to listen for the sound /ă/.
4. Stress that the sound heard is called the short sound of *a.* Have the children note how this sound differs from the letter name.
5. Ask students how many vowels they see in each word and where the vowel is located (middle of the word).

6. Have children state what sound is heard when there is one vowel in the middle of a word.[1]
7. Have children state in their own words the rule that covers this vowel situation.

Using this approach, the following generalization will evolve: "One vowel in the middle of the word usually has its short sound." It is probably not essential that each child be able to recite all the generalizations in this chapter. At this point, it might be profitable to cite other familiar words that follow the generalizations under discussion, even though all the stimulus words are not yet known as sight words.

Using Word Families

Some teachers find that certain children can do better in fixing the short sound of a given vowel if they see and pronounce a series of words that contain larger identical units than the vowel alone: the words *big, ship, tin,* and *hill* have an identical unit—*i.* The words *big, pig, dig,* and *fig,* and *hill, fill, bill,* and *pill,* and *sit, fit, bit,* and *kit* have rhyming units composed of several letters that have precisely the same phonic value in each word. Word families can be used both for teaching common phonic elements and for rapid recognition as sight words.

To teach the phonogram *ad,* you might begin with these words: *dad, had, sad, mad, bad,* and *lad.* Use the seven steps previously outlined to teach this and other identical phonogram words.

1. Pronounce each word; have children pronounce the words.
2. Stress the vowel sound heard and the visual pattern: one vowel, medial position.

Sample words follow for the vowels *e, i, o,* and *u.* The first column under each vowel includes words with mixed initial and final consonants; the second column presents the same final phonogram (letter-pattern) in each word.

e		i		o		u	
red	jet	big	hit	hop	cot	bus	bug
let	pet	tin	bit	job	not	run	rug
bell	let	hill	sit	stop	hot	cup	hug
send	bet	did	pit	log	pot	jump	jug
men	met	pig	fit	box	got	cut	mug
step	set	lift	lit	rock	lot	must	tug

[1]Strictly speaking, the vowel in words such as *back, bank,* and *trap* is not in the middle of the word. Children are usually not confused by this statement, but you can modify the generalization if you wish.

USING CONTEXT

Teacher: "Read the clue. Use one of the vowel letters *a, e,* or *o* to spell the word that fits the clue."

Example:

Clue

spider   w____b   use *e* to spell *web*
angry   m____d   use *a* to spell *mad*
horses   tr____t   use *o* to spell *trot*

	Clue				*Clue*	
1.	fishing	n____t		**6.**	soda	p____p
2.	chicken	h____n		**7.**	number	t____n
3.	steal	r____b		**8.**	floor	l____mp
4.	bird's	n____st		**9.**	cry	s____b
5.	paper	b____g		**10.**	lion's	d____n

Teacher: "Use one of the vowel letters *i, u,* or *e* to spell the word."

	Clue				*Clue*	
1.	chewy	g____m		**6.**	fish	sw____m
2.	color	r____d		**7.**	scissors	c____t
3.	tops	sp____n		**8.**	rings	b____ll
4.	plane	j____t		**9.**	fruit	pl____m
5.	ruler	k____ng		**10.**	large	b____g

Teacher: "Read the clue. Write the vowel that completes the word that fits the clue."

Example:
you sleep on this   b____d (e)

Clue			*Clue*	
it's large	b____g		can ring it	b____ll
paper sack	b____g		can throw it	b____ll
an insect	b____g		lives on a farm	b____ll
to keep asking for	b____g		a boy's name	B____ll

Teacher: "Read the clue. Write the word that fits the clue."

Example:
The pig is in the _____ .   (pin, pen)

Clue
Do you like corn on the _____?   (cab, cob)
John said, "I can read the _____ ."   (mop, map)
The cat drank milk from the _____ .   (cap, cup)
Cats and dogs are _____ .   (pots, pets)
A baby bear is a _____ .   (cab, cub)

Teacher: "Each sentence has two blanks. One of the words *pig* or *pen* will fit in each space. Study each sentence and write the correct words."

Example:
The (*pig*) is in the (*pen*).

1. Put the _____ in the _____ .
2. Will the _____ hold the _____ ?
3. The _____ will hold the _____ .
4. The _____ should be in the _____ .
5. The _____ is for the _____ .
6. Is the _____ in the _____ ?
7. The _____ belongs in the _____ .
8. It is time to _____ up the _____ .

Teacher: "Read each sentence. One of the words at the right fits in the blank space. The only difference in the words is the vowel letter. Write the correct word in the blank space."

Example:
The _____ was many years old.   click
                                                    clock

1. There was a _____ on the beach.   crab
                                                            crib

2. The _____ was full of coal.   trick
                                                        truck

3. John was able to _____ the word.   spell
                                                             spill

4. Spot is a _____ dog.   smell
                                                 small

5. _____ the letter in the mailbox.   Drop

Drip

FUN WITH LANGUAGE

Teacher: "Fill every blank space with a vowel. The context will help you pick the right vowel."

Clue: <u>Suzy sings a lot.</u>

Will she sing a song again if she has just sung that song?

1. Just ask Suzy and she will s_____ ng any s_____ ng.

2. Once she s_____ ng a very pretty s_____ ng.

3. Later, someone asked her to s_____ ng that s_____ ng again.

4. She said, "I just s_____ ng that s_____ ng."

5. I should not s_____ ng a s_____ ng that I have just s_____ ng.

6. Was Suzy right not to s_____ ng that s_____ ng again?

7. Would you s_____ ng a s_____ ng you had just s_____ ng?

8. If you have just s_____ ng a s_____ ng and you want to s_____ ng it again, s_____ng it!

BUCKETS AND BLANK SPACES

Teacher: "Note that each word with a blank in it has the same three letters. To complete each word, you must add a vowel. Which vowel goes where? As you read the sentence, the context will indicate where to add *a, e, i,* and *u.*"

1. First, you f_____ ll the bucket f_____ ll of water.

2. Don't f_____ ll while carrying a bucket f_____ ll of water.

3. If you f_____ ll, the bucket might not be f_____ ll.

4. He f_____ ll, then he had to f_____ ll the bucket again.

5. Don't f_____ ll if you want a f_____ ll bucket.

Teacher: "In each of the following sentences, two words need a vowel. The context will help you decide which words fit. Write the vowel letter to complete each word."

Set 1

Use only the vowels *u, i,* and *e.*

1. Is the b_____ g very b_____ g?

2. S_____ t the basket down and come s_____ t by me.

3. Don't d_____ g where we d_____ g yesterday.

4. That t_____ n cup cost t_____ n cents.

5. She asked h_____ m, "Can you h_____ m this song?"

6. You write with a p_____ n, not with a p_____ n.

Set 2

Use only the vowels *a, o,* and *i.*

1. The c_____ t was asleep on the c_____ t.

2. "Watch out," said Joe, "the p_____ t is very h_____ t."

3. I want to s_____ t where we s_____ t yesterday.

4. Ask h_____ m if he wants a h_____ m sandwich.

5. Put the b_____ g dish in the paper b_____ g.

6. When the weather is h_____ t you should wear a h_____ t.

Minimal Contrast Vowels

Practice in associating vowel letter forms with the short sounds they represent can be presented in many ways. The examples start with contrasting two vowel sounds and gradually move through all vowels in medial position.

Contrasting two vowel sounds. As soon as two vowel sounds have been introduced, the difference between them can be stressed.

1. Write pairs of words on the chalkboard.

bat—bet	mat—met	pat—pet	sat—set
man—men	tan—ten	bad—bed	lad—led

2. Pronounce these words, inviting children to listen to the difference in the vowel sounds heard in the middle of the words.
3. Have children pronounce the pairs of words, noting each vowel letter form and the sound it represents.

The short sounds of *e* and *i* often pose special difficulty because of either poor auditory discrimination or dialectical differences in pronunciation. The following pairs of words, identical except for the vowel *i* or *e,* can be used in both auditory and visual drill.

led—lid	big—beg	pig—peg	wit—wet
pin—pen	tin—ten	din—den	met—mitt
bed—bid	pep—pip	bet—bit	rid—red
lit—let	pit—pet	sit—set	hem—him

Various exercises using different modes of presentation can be built from pairs of words such as these.

u, i	*u, e*	*a, u*	*o, u*
bug—big	bug—beg	bag—bug	cot—cut
but—bit	but—bet	bat—but	hot—hut
hut—hit	nut—net	cat—cut	not—nut
dug—dig	hum—hem	cap—cup	hog—hug

e, o	*a, o*	*a, i*	*i, o*
get—got	cat—cot	lap—lip	hip—hop
let—lot	hat—hot	nap—nip	tip—top
net—not	pat—pot	rap—rip	Tim—Tom
pet—pot	rat—rot	tap—tip	hit—hot

Seeing and sounding drill. After all short vowel letter-sounds have been introduced, exercise material can help children fix the visual-auditory relationship involved in the single-vowel-in-medial-position generalization. To use the following material, children should be told that the words in each line are exactly the same except for the vowel letter-sound.

1. "Listen for the difference (vowel sound) in each word."
2. "If the word is underlined, it is a nonsense word you haven't met—but you still can pronounce it."
3. "Read across each line of words."

a	*e*	*i*	*o*	*u*
bag	beg	big	bog	bug
→	→	→	→	
lad	led	lid	<u>lod</u>	<u>lud</u>
pat	pet	pit	pot	<u>pud</u>
<u>dask</u>	desk	disk	<u>dosk</u>	dusk
jag	<u>jeg</u>	jig	jog	jug
ham	hem	him	<u>hom</u>	hum
fan	<u>fen</u>	fin	<u>fon</u>	fun
Nat	net	nit	not	nut
lack	<u>leck</u>	lick	lock	luck
sap	<u>sep</u>	sip	sop	sup

BLEND AND SAY

Teacher: "Each word has a blank space. A vowel letter is shown above each blank space. Think of the sound of the vowel letter and say each word."

a	e	i	o	u
b____t	b____d	h____t	h____p	f____n

a	e	i	o	u
c____n	j____t	p____g	l____g	b____s

e	u	o	i	a
m____n	g____m	c____t	s____x	f____t

i	o	a	u	e
d____g	m____p	r____t	f____n	l____g

 CHANGE THE VOWEL

Teacher: "Change the vowel and make a naming word for something living using the vowels *a, e, i, o,* or *u.*"

Examples:

cot—cat

pep—pup

dig	d____g	big	b____g
dock	d____ck	limb	l____mb
pit	p____t	crib	cr____b
cot	c____t	bell	b____ll
fix	f____x	peg	p____g

 WRITE AND SAY

This material can be presented in many different ways, including the chalkboard and duplicated exercises.

Teacher: "Put the vowel *a* in each of the following blank spaces. Then pronounce the word."

t____p	b____d
n____p	d____d
l____p	h____d
m____p	m____d
c____p	s____d

Teacher: "Put the vowel *e* in each of the following blank spaces. Then pronounce the word."

m____n	l___t
p____n	n___t
d____n	p___t
h____n	j___t
t____n	b___t

Teacher: "Put the vowel *i* in each of the following blank spaces. Pronounce the word."

p____n	h___t
t____n	b___t
b____n	s___t
f____n	f___t
s____n	p___t

Teacher: "Put the vowel *u* in each of the following blank spaces. Pronounce the word."

r____g	r____n
j____g	s____n
h____g	f____n
t____g	g____n
d____g	b____n

Teacher: "Add a vowel to make a word. Only one vowel fits in each word."

Examples:

w____b   (e)   *a, e, i, o, u*
f____sh   (i)

1. y____s	**7.** gl____d	**13.** k____ss
2. v____m	**8.** c____n	**14.** pl____n
3. sw____n	**9.** y____t	**15.** b____s
4. cl____b	**10.** s____ch	**16.** m____lk
5. r____ch	**11.** d____st	**17.** s____nt
6. k____g	**12.** d____t	**18.** n____st

Combining Teaching of Initial and Medial Vowel Sounds

Some teachers prefer to teach the short sound of initial and medial vowels simultaneously. The procedure can be much the same as for the medial-vowel situation;

however, the generalization that emerges will be stated differently. To illustrate this concept, place a number of stimulus words on the board.

a	*a*
am	ham
ask	task
at	bat
and	sand
as	gas
act	fact
an	pan

Words in the first column contain one initial vowel, and the short sound is heard. Words in the second column contain one medial vowel, and the short sound is heard. As children see and hear the letter-sound relationship, the generalization will emerge: "When the only vowel in a word does not come at the end of the word, it usually has its short sound."

LONG VOWEL (GLIDED) LETTER-SOUNDS

In teaching the long vowel letter-sounds, keep in mind that children differentiate these sounds when they process or use oral language. In the reading process, teaching the long vowel letter-sounds focuses primarily on having children recognize several visual patterns and associate these with the sounds they characteristically represent.

Using Visual Patterns as Cues to Sounding

Despite the large number of exceptions to any generalizations advanced to cover vowel letter-sounds, certain visual cues must be heeded. We will look at the following major patterns.

Two adjacent vowels (particularly m*ee*t, s*ea*t, c*oa*t, s*ai*l)

Medial vowel and final *e* (r*o*p*e*, c*a*p*e*, c*u*t*e*, t*i*r*e*)

Single vowel that concludes a word (g*o*, m*e*)

How *y* functions at the end of words (m*y*, ma*y*)

Two adjacent vowels are covered by this generalization: "When two vowels come together, the first one usually has its long sound and the second is not sounded."

Data from studies of a large sample of words met in elementary reading materials indicate that this generalization actually applies to less than half the words that meet the two-vowel criterion; however, the generalization held fairly consistently for the *ee*, *oa*, *ai*, and *ea* patterns. Studies revealed the percentage of instances in which the two-vowel rule applies: *ee*, 98%; *oa*, 97%; *ai*, 64%; *ea*, 66%; and all two-vowel situations combined, 48% (Oaks, 1952; Clymer, 1963).

In the following examples, teaching does not start with a statement of generalizations, but with material that emphasizes the visual patterns *oa, ee, ai, ea.* The patterns are linked to the sound heard in words and permit the children to discover the relationship and arrive at the generalization.

1. Place a column of *oa* words on the board: *boat, coat, load, road,* and *soak.*
2. Pronounce each word, emphasizing the long /ō/ sound.
3. Have children note the visual pattern of the two vowels.
4. Point out that in each word you hear the long sound of the first vowel and the second vowel is not sounded. This may be illustrated, as in the right-hand column.

boat	bōa̸t
coat	cōa̸t
load	lōa̸d
road	rōa̸d
soak	sōa̸k

A similar procedure can be followed to introduce the patterns *ai, ea,* and *ee.*

ai		*ea*		*ee*	
chain	chāi̸n	beat	bēa̸t	feed	fēe̸d
mail	māi̸l	dream	drēa̸m	seed	sēe̸d
wait	wāi̸t	leaf	lēa̸f	keep	kēe̸p
rain	rāi̸n	teach	tēa̸ch	queen	quēe̸n
paid	pāi̸d	seat	sēa̸t	steel	stēe̸l

Teaching Short and Long Sounds Together

Some teachers prefer to present short and long sounds simultaneously. This procedure permits children to see both patterns (single and double vowel letters) and to contrast the sounds in familiar words. Material can be presented in two- or three-step fashion.

Teacher: "Today we want to practice hearing the difference between two sounds of the vowel letter *a.* In the first column, each word has one vowel letter. In the second column, each word has two vowels together."

ran	rain
pad	paid
bat	bait
lad	laid
pal	pail
mad	maid
pan	pain

1. Pronounce the words in the first column; then have the children read these words.
2. Have children note the following.
   a. Each word has one vowel.
   b. The vowel is in the middle of the word.
   c. The short sound /ă/ of the vowel is heard.
3. Repeat the procedure for the words in the second column, having children note the following.
   a. Each word contains the vowel pattern *ai*.
   b. They say and hear the letter *a* /ā/.
   c. They do not sound or hear the second vowel letter.

   The three-step approach permits children to see the process of adding a second vowel. This produces a new word containing two vowels that represent the long vowel sound heard.

One Vowel	Add i	New Word	
ă	↓	ā	
ran	ra*i*n	rā*i*n	(second vowel
pad	pa d	pāid	not sounded)
bat	ba t	bāit	
lad	la d	lāid	
pal	pa l	pāil	
mad	ma d	māid	
pan	pa n	pāin	

These words can be used to teach the other two-vowel patterns, *ee, ea,* and *oa.*

ă	ē¢	ĕ	ēa̸	ŏ	ōa
bet	beet	set	seat	cot	coat
met	meet	men	mean	got	goat
fed	feed	bet	beat	rod	road
step	steep	bed	bead	Tod	toad
pep	peep	met	meat	cost	coast

❧ USING CONTEXT

Teacher: "Read the clue. Complete the word that fits the clue. Use one of the vowel patterns *a—e, i—e,* or *o—e* to spell the word."

Example:

Clue

Opening in fence	g____t____	(*a—e* for *gate*)
A pretty flower	r____s____	(*o—e* for *rose*)

Clue		*Clue*	
ten cents	d____m____	sticky stuff	p____st____
a brief letter	n____t____	a two-wheeler	b____k____
a number	n____n____	a body of water	l____k____
glass in window	p____n____	a funny story	j____k____
where there's fire	sm____k____	go fly a	k____t____

Teacher: "Use one of the vowel patterns *ai, ee,* or *ea* to spell the word."

Clue		*Clue*	
used for thinking	br____n	a lady ruler	qu____n
falls from clouds	r____n	when it hurts	p____n
a vegetable	b____t	path in woods	tr____l
to cure the sick	h____l	along the ocean	b____ch
not very strong	w____k	back of foot	h____l

Teacher: "The two words *not* and *note* fit in the two blanks in each sentence. Study each sentence and fill in the blanks."

1. He did _____ see the _____ .

2. The _____ was _____ seen.

3. Why did he _____ see the _____?

4. Was the _____ seen or _____?

5. No, the _____ was _____ seen.

Teacher: "One of the words *met* or *meet* will fit in each blank space. Complete each sentence."

Examples:

Did you _____meet_____ the new teacher?

Yes, we _____met_____ yesterday.

1. _____ me at the ball game.

2. They _____ last year at camp.

3. The boys _____ at the track _____ .

4. She will _____ us at four o'clock.

5. He said, " _____ me where we _____ last time."

Teacher: "All these sentences contain two blank spaces. Each word following a sentence will fit in one blank space. You decide which one."

Example:

When the _____rain_____ started, he _____ran_____ home.   ran

                                                                          rain

1. They _____ at the _____ market.   met

                                                                          meat

2. Some of the _____ were _____ .   mean

                                                                          men

3. Do not _____ it where you _____ it before.   hid

                                                                          hide

4. The doctor said, "You _____ walk with a _____ ."   cane

                                                                          can

5. She _____ some of the people _____ .   mad

                                                                          made

FUN WITH LANGUAGE

Teacher: "In each sentence, three words need a pair of vowels. Write *ee, ea,* or *oa* in each blank space."

1. T_____ch children to k_____p off the r_____d.
2. You don't f_____d m_____t to a g_____t.
3. We n_____d a r_____l rain to s_____k the ground.
4. It's hard to k_____p a c_____l mine cl_____n.
5. We n_____d some m_____t and a l_____f of bread.
6. I f_____l like having r_____st beef and pie with my m_____l.
7. It was m_____n to k_____p the g_____t tied up.

Teacher: "Each of the following sentences contains two words with missing vowels. The clue tells you which vowel patterns will fit. Read the sentence to learn where they fit."

Set 1

Clues to Use: ee, oa, *and* ea

1. M_____t me at the m_____t market.
2. He sat near the r_____d to r_____d his book.
3. The doctor said, "This will h_____l your injured h_____l.
4. She took a last p_____k at the high mountain p_____k.

Set 2

Clues to Use: ea, ai, *and* oa

1. If we s____l to the island we may see the s____l.
2. The guide said, "Put the b____t in the b____t."
3. The g____t walked with a funny g____t.
4. Is the r____l made of r____l walnut wood?

Two Vowels, One of Which Is Final *e*

The generalization for this C-V-C-V pattern is "In words with two vowels, the second being final *e*, the first vowel usually has its long sound and the final *e* is not sounded." Clymer (1963) found that the pronunciation of 60% of the final-e words in his sample were governed by this generalization. Again, material can be presented so that children see the pattern, hear the long vowel sound, and arrive at the generalization.

1. Write on the board words that have a single vowel in medial position. Choose words to which a final *e* may be added to form a new word.
2. In an adjacent column, print these final-e words.
3. Have children pronounce these pairs of words, listening to the difference in the vowel sounds.

Stress the visual pattern vowel + *e*, and guide children in verbalizing the generalization: "In words with two vowels, the second being final *e*, the final *e* is not sounded and the first vowel usually has its long sound." You can use diacritical marks as shown in column C.

A	B	C
hat	hate	hātͤ
hid	hide	hīdͤ
past	paste	pāstͤ
pal	pale	pālͤ
cut	cute	cūtͤ
plan	plane	plānͤ
rat	rate	rātͤ
pin	pine	pīnͤ
strip	stripe	strīpͤ
rid	ride	rīdͤ

FUN WITH LANGUAGE

Teacher: "In each sentence, two words need a vowel. The same vowel letter fits in both blanks. One word will have its short sound; the other will have the long sound. Write in the vowel that makes sense."

1. John said, "I would h_____ te to lose my new h_____ t."
2. Do n_____ t forget to leave a n_____ te.
3. I h_____ pe the rabbit will not h_____ p on the flowers.
4. His friend P_____ te has a p_____ t turtle.
5. A r_____ t can run at a very fast r_____ te.
6. Their job was to c_____ t out some c_____ te cartoons.
7. Under the p_____ ne tree, he found a pretty p_____ n.
8. If you h_____ d there once, don't h_____ de there again.

Teacher: "Every word with a blank space ends with a silent *e*. Each blank space needs a vowel. This vowel will have its long vowel sound. Complete all of the words so that each sentence makes sense."

1. D_____ ve, M_____ ke, and K_____ te m_____ de plans for a picnic.
2. M_____ke will b_____ke a c_____ke.
3. K_____te will t_____ke a l_____me-and-lemon drink.
4. D_____ve will t_____ke a pl_____te of r_____pe fruit.
5. Later, D_____ve and M_____ke met K_____te at the l_____ke.
6. She r_____de her b_____ke; she l_____kes to r_____de it.
7. They will w_____de in the l_____ke, then t_____ke a h_____ke.

Single Final Vowels

When the only vowel in a word comes at the end of the word, it usually has its long sound. There probably are enough high-frequency words covered by this generalization to justify calling it to children's attention.

1. Place on the board words that contain one vowel in final position.
2. Have the children pronounce each word, noting the vowel at the end of the word and the sound it represents.
3. Invite children to supply a generalization covering these words (one final vowel has the long sound).

we	no
be	go
me	so
she	
he	

Notable exceptions to this generalization include *do, to, who,* and *two.* In words that end with *y* and that contain no other vowel, the *y* functions as a vowel. In these words the *y* is sounded as long /ī/ (*my, by, try, fly, cry, dry, sky, shy*).

At the end of words,* ay *has the sound of long /ā/.   Children have learned that *y* functions as a vowel when it ends a word that has no other vowel letter. Here they learn that *y* following the vowel *a* fits a generalization learned previously: "When two vowels come together, the first usually has its long sound."

1. Place a few stimulus words on the board.
2. Lead the children in pronouncing these words.
3. Focus attention on the visual pattern *ay* and on the resulting sound of long /ā/.
4. Other words that fit this pattern: *play, hay, ray, pray, sway, jay, stray, gray, away,* and *tray.*

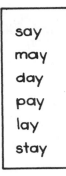

Sound of* y *at the end of longer words.   When *y* concludes a word of two or more syllables, it has the long sound of /ē/ heard in hob*by,* win*dy,* fog*gy,* luc*ky,* jol*ly,* fun*ny,* hap*py,* mer*ry,* nois*y,* and rus*ty.* Other words to use in teaching exercises are *badly, angry, plenty, honestly, closely, beauty, mainly, guilty, history, lively, nasty, January, partly, ready, seventy, rocky, penny, muddy, simply, sorry, jelly, nearly, costly,* and *sleepy.*

EXCEPTIONS TO VOWEL RULES PREVIOUSLY TAUGHT

There is no vowel rule or generalization that will apply in all situations. When exceptions to a given rule occur, they may be taught as sight words, or a new rule can be devised to cover the exception. It has been suggested that children not be burdened with rules that have limited applications. Different teachers will, of course, arrive at different conclusions as to which generalizations should be included in phonics instruction. Some exceptions to a given rule occur with such frequency as to merit calling children's attention to the exceptions.

For instance, one of the most useful phonic generalizations we have discussed states: "One vowel in medial position usually has its short sound." There are several series of words that meet the criterion of one vowel in medial position but in which the vowel has its long sound. For example, the vowel *o* followed by *ld* or *lt* usually has the long sound: *bold, mold, gold, sold, hold, told, fold, cold, colt, bolt, volt,* and *jolt.* Also, the vowel *i* followed by *nd, gh,* or *ld* frequently has the long sound: *find, blind, behind, mind, kind, light, fight, sight, right, wild, mild,* and *child.*

Two Adjacent Vowels

The generalization covering two adjacent vowels ("The first usually has its long sound; the second is not sounded") has some exceptions in the patterns *oa, ai, ee,* and *ea.* While children are learning the words that follow the rule, they should also understand that exceptions will occur, such as *been, again, against, aisle, said, bread, break, head, dead, heart, steak,* and *broad.* There are many more exceptions found among other two-vowel patterns, including the following.

ei	ou	ie	au	ui, -ue, -ua
their	could	chief	caught	build
weigh	enough	field	laugh	guide
eight	rough	friend	fault	quiet
neighbor	should	piece	haunt	guess
vein	would	quiet	taught	guest
freight	touch	view	daughter	guard
rein	double	believe	haul	usual

Medial Vowel Plus Final *e*

Since a number of frequently met words, particularly *o* + *e* words, do not follow the generalization that one vowel in medial position usually has its short sound, some teachers prefer to deal with this fact rather than ignore it. Teachers might point out several exceptions, noting that applying the generalization will not help in solving the words *come, done, none, move, have, were, there, one, some, gone, love, glove, give, sense, where,* and *lose.*

VOWEL SOUNDS AFFECTED BY *R*

A vowel (or vowels) followed by the letter *r* results in a blended sound that is neither the short nor the long sound of the vowel. This phonic fact—as it relates to learning to read—is probably not extremely important; however, calling children's attention to this role of the letter *r* is a justifiable procedure. Since children use and understand hundreds of words that include a vowel followed by *r*, this is not a particularly difficult fact to teach. More important, children will have mastered several such words as sight words, and these can serve as examples when the generalization is introduced.

Following are some of the more common vowel -*r* words for use in board work or seatwork exercises.

-*ar*		-*er*	-*or*
car	yard	her	for
farm	park	person	corn
march	card	term	storm
part	far	serve	horn
star	smart	ever	short
dark	arm	certain	north
hard	bark	berth	horse
barn	tar	herd	corner
start	spark	under	form

The spelling *ir* is usually pronounced *ûr* (bird = bûrd), except when followed by a final *e* (fire): *bird, dirt, firm, third, fir, thirst, girl, first, sir, shirt, birth,* and *stir.*

A FOLLOWED BY *L, LL, W,* AND *U*

The letter *a* has the sound /ô/ (*aw*) when it is followed by *l, ll, w,* or *u.* For example:

talk	all	wall	saw	claw	haul
walk	tall	fall	draw	straw	because
salt	small	call	lawn	drawn	fault
halt	hall	ball	drawn	jaw	Paul

THE *OO* SOUNDS

Explaining the sounds of *oo* is much more complicated than actually learning to arrive at the correct pronunciation of the frequently used words that contain this letter combination. Most words containing *oo* are pronounced in one of two ways:

With the sound heard in *boo* and *boot*

With the sound heard in *book* and *foot*

Native speakers of English do not confuse these sounds while speaking or listening. When reading for meaning, children will not confuse the medial sounds heard in the two words used in each of these sentences:

The boot is larger than the foot.

The food is very good.

Beginning readers may not consciously note that the sounds are different because they never substitute one for the other. Practice in hearing differences can be provided by having children tell which of the following pairs of words rhyme.

cool—pool	food—good	soon—moon
boot—foot	book—look	look—hook
hoot—foot	wood—good	boot—hoot

The markings $\overline{oo}$ and $o\breve{o}$ may help children note the differences between these sounds, as in these sentences.

The bo͞ot is larger than the fo͝ot.

The mo͞ose drank from the co͞ol po͞ol.

He to͝ok a lo͝ok at the bro͝ok.

In the final analysis, it is the context that helps children arrive at the correct pronunciation. For convenience in creating board or seatwork exercises, here are some $\overline{oo}$ and $o\breve{o}$ words:

$\overline{oo}$					$o\breve{o}$	
bo͞o	soon	moon	boost		book	fo͝ot
cool	tool	broom	loop		good	to͝ok
food	boot	pool	hoot		stood	lo͝ok
room	boon	loose	moose		shook	crook
tooth	zoo	root	proof		wood	hook

A few *oo* words are neither $\overline{oo}$ or $o\breve{o}$, such as *blood* (blŭd), *door* (dōr), *flood* (flŭd), and *floor* (flōr). These should be taught as sight words.

DIPHTHONGS

A diphthong is two adjacent vowels, each of which contributes to the sound heard. The diphthongs discussed here are *ou, oi,* and *oy.* In pronouncing diphthongs, the two vowel sounds are blended, as in *house, oil,* and *boy.*

1. The diphthongs *oi* and *oy* have the same sound (boy = bo*i*; boil = bo*i*l).
2. Sometimes *ow* represents the diphthong sound of *ou.*

Diphthong Sounds

1. Place several words on the board that illustrate the diphthong sound *oy* (column A).
2. In column B, change the spelling to *oi*, and in column C, add a final consonant to form a known word.

A		B		C
boy	→	boi	→	boil
toy	→	toi	→	toil
joy	→	joi	→	join
coy	→	coi	→	coin

3. Pronounce the words across each line, emphasizing that the *oy* and *oi* spellings represent the same sounds.
4. Point out that each vowel contributes to the sound heard.
5. Have children note that these vowel patterns do not follow the generalization that the first vowel has its long sound, and the second is not sounded.

   Teaching that *ou* and *ow* represent the same sound may be done as follows.

1. Have children pronounce these pairs of words, noting that *ou* and *ow* represent the same sound.

*ow*l	*fou*l
cr*ow*d	cl*ou*d
f*ow*l	gr*ou*nd

2. Place other *ou* and *ow* stimulus words on the board. In pronouncing the words in columns A and B, help children note that the letters *ou* and *ow* represent the same sound.

A	B
how	out
howl	foul
town	found
drown	ground
clown	round
crown	sound

Words to use in board or seatwork drill include the following:

cow	owl	mouse	mouth	boil	boy
how	gown	sound	proud	coin	toy
brown	howl	loud	shout	toil	oyster
tower	brow	couch	found	joint	joy
crown	town	south	count	soil	Troy
powder	fowl	ground	bound	moist	employ

ow as the Long Sound of *o*

In a number of English words, the *ow* combination has the sound of /ō/. You can use the following steps to teach the sound.

1. The letter combination *ow* has two sounds: the diphthong sound heard in *plow* and the /ō/ heard in *snow.*

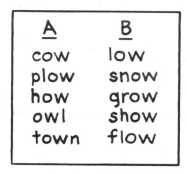

2. Pronounce the words in column A, with the children listening to the sound of */ow/.*
3. Pronounce pairs of words (cow, low) with the children listening to contrasting sounds.
4. Have the children pronounce the words.
5. Point out that as words are read in context, the proper sound becomes obvious because the children know these words.

HOMONYMS

Homonyms are words that have the same pronunciation but different spellings and meanings. These words involve both structural and phonic analysis skills. Some homonyms follow one of the generalizations we have already introduced; many do not. For example, the rule "When two vowels occur together, the first is long, and the second is not sounded" applies to both words in the following pairs: *meet, meat; see, sea;* and *week, weak.*

Sometimes the rule applies to one word in a pair, and the final -e rule applies to the other word: *road, rode; sail, sale;* and *pain, pane.*

Some pairs involve unsounded consonants: *rap, wrap; new, knew;* and *our, hour.*

Other examples of phonic irregularities are *wait, weight; wood, would; ate, eight;* and *piece, peace.* The following exercises may be used or adapted to help children recognize homonyms that have irregular spellings.

WORKING WITH HOMONYMS

1. Recognizing Homonyms

Directions: Explain the concept of homonyms: words that are pronounced the same but have different spellings and meanings. Have children pronounce the pairs of words at the left and answer the questions by writing *yes* or *no.*

	Same Spelling?	*Same Sound?*
there—their		
ate—eight		
two—to		
would—wood		
one—won		
I—eye		
some—sum		
by—buy		
our—hour		
do—due		

2. Matching Homonyms

Directions: Draw a line from the word in column A to the word in column B that is pronounced the same.

A	B	A	B
won	no	knot	blew
know	sew	blue	maid
so	one	made	not
pole	some	son	I
hour	eight	eye	sea
ate	our	pear	sun
sum	poll	see	pare

3. Match and Write Homonyms

Directions: Explain that each word in the clue box is pronounced like one of the words below the box. Children are to write the correct word on each blank space.

Clue Box							
eight	one	weigh	sew	some	would	wait	hole

so _____   ate _____

won _____   sum _____

way _____   wood _____

whole _____   weight _____

These are some common homonyms to use in board or seatwork exercises.

beat—beet	maid—made	pair—pare
know—no	I—eye	mail—male
hear—here	hair—hare	steel—steal
there—their	by—buy	waist—waste
sun—son	fair—fare	one—won
whole—hole	dear—deer	some—sum
oh—owe	not—knot	tail—tale

USING CONTEXT

Teacher: "Two words follow each clue. These are homonyms: words pronounced the same but spelled differently. Read the clue and write the correct word in the blank space."

Example:

big price cut   _____ sale _____   sail   sale

	Clue			
1.	the ears do it	_____	here	hear
2.	part of a window	_____	pain	pane
3.	seven days in a	_____	week	weak
4.	the eyes do it	_____	sea	see
5.	an odd-shaped fruit	_____	pair	pear
6.	fuel for a fireplace	_____	wood	would
7.	a vegetable	_____	beat	beet
8.	top of a mountain	_____	peek	peak
9.	back part of the foot	_____	heal	heel
10.	cars move on it	_____	rode	road

Teacher: "One of the words *weak* or *week* will fit in each blank space. Study each sentence and fill in the blanks."

Example:

There are seven days in a _____ . (week)

He felt very _____ after the fever. (weak)

1. John was sick last _____ .

2. He feels _____ this _____ .

3. John has felt _____ since last _____ .

4. Next _____ , John will not be _____ .

5. How did John feel last _____?

Teacher: "Each sentence has an underlined word and a blank space. In the blank space, write a homonym for the underlined word."

Examples:

We can be at <u>our</u> house in an _____ . (hour)

Who <u>knew</u> about the _____ plans? (new)

1. The team <u>won</u> only _____ game.

2. <u>Eight</u> of the boys _____ all of the chicken.

3. _____ house is over <u>there</u>.

4. <u>Would</u> you please bring in some _____ .

5. You can _____ the ocean if you come over <u>here</u>.

Teacher: "Each of these sentences has two missing words. The words *our* and *hour* will fit in each sentence. Where does each word fit?"

Example:

There was a one _____ meeting at _____ house.

Teacher: "Using the context of the sentence you would write:

There was a one *hour* meeting at *our* house."

1. _____ game will start in one _____ .

2. In about an _____ _____ game will start.

3. Will it take an _____ to play _____ game?

4. We can play _____ game in less than an _____ .

Teacher: "The words *mail* and *male* are homonyms. Homonyms are words that are pronounced the same, but have different meanings. Each of these sentences has two missing words. The words *mail* and *male* will fit in each sentence. Where does each word fit?"

Example:

A _____ or a female may bring the _____ .

Teacher: "Note that the context helps you get it right.

A *male* or a female may bring the *mail.*"

1. When a _____ delivers the _____ he is called a mailman.
2. A _____ delivering the _____ is not a "maleman."
3. _____ can be delivered by a _____ or a female.
4. Who is the _____ delivering the _____ today?
5. That _____ delivering the _____ is Charlie.

THE SCHWA SOUND

In a large number of words of more than one syllable, there is a diminished stress on one of the syllables. The sound of the vowel in these unstressed syllables undergoes a slight change, referred to as a "softening" of the vowel sound. This softened vowel sound is called the *schwa* sound, and it is represented by the symbol ə.

All of the vowels are represented by the schwa sound, as illustrated by each of the italicized vowels in these words.

bedl*a*m	=	bed'ləm
beat*e*n	=	bē'tən
beaut*i*ful	=	bū'tə fəl
beck*o*n	=	bek'ən

In other words, if vowels were interchanged in unstressed syllables, the spellings would change, but the sound heard would remain the same for the different vowels. For instance, read both of these sentences without stressing the second syllable in any word.

    A. Button, button, who has the button?

    B. Buttun, buttan, who has the butten?

If, in reading sentence B, you give each second syllable the same stress as it was given in the word directly above it, the sounds remain constant. Thus, teaching the schwa sound in the initial stages of reading would have little impact on one's ability to sound out words. Once the child begins to use a dictionary that utilizes the schwa symbol ə, however, these points should be explained.

SIGHT-WORD LIST

Table 6–1 is a list of words, most of which are met in primary reading, that illustrates irregular spellings. From the standpoint of spoken language, all words are phonetic; however, the spellings (visual patterns) of these words are such that the more common phonic generalizations learned in beginning reading will not apply.

TABLE 6–1 *Sight-Word List: Words with Irregular Spellings Resulting in Confusion Between Letters Seen and Sounds Heard*

above	could	ghost	love	quiet	together
across	couple	give			ton
again	cousin	gives	machine	ranger	tongue
against	cruel	gloves	many	ready	too
aisle	curve	gone	measure	really	touch
already		great	might	right	two
another	dead	guard	mild	rough	
answer	deaf	guess	million		use
anxious	debt	guest	mind	said	usual
any	desire	guide	minute	says	
	do		mischief	school	vein
bear	does	have	mother	science	very
beautiful	done	head	move	scissors	view
beauty	don't	heart	Mr.	sew	
because	double	heaven	Mrs.	shoe	was
been	doubt	heavy		should	wash
behind	dove	here	neighbor	sign	weather
believe	dozen	high	neither	snow	weight
bind			night	soften	were
both	early	idea	none	soldier	what
bough	earn	Indian		some	where
bread	eight	instead	ocean	someone	who
break	enough	isle	of	something	whom
bright	eye		office	sometime	whose
brought	eyes	key	often	son	wild
build		kind	oh	soul	wind
built	father	knee	once	special	wolf
bury	fence	knew	one	spread	woman
busy	field	knife	onion	square	women
buy	fight	know	only	steak	won
	find		other	straight	would
calf	folks	language	ought	sure	wrong
captain	four	laugh		sword	
caught	freight	laughed	patient		you
chief	friend	leather	piece	their	young
child	front	library	pretty	there	your
clothes		light	pull	they	
colt	garage	lion	purpose	though	
coming	get	live	push	thought	
cough	getting	lived	put	to	

SUMMARY

There is considerable variability in the sounds of vowels and vowel combinations in English. This increases the difficulty of teaching or learning vowel sounds. The sequence in which vowel sounds are taught—that is, whether to teach long or short sounds first or which vowels to teach first—is probably not a significant issue. The teaching procedures in this chapter are meant to be illustrative rather than prescriptive.

Some generalizations covering vowel situations include the following:

- A single vowel in medial position in a word or syllable usually has its short sound (man, bed, fit).
- When two vowels are side by side in a word, the first usually has its long sound and the second is not sounded.
- When a word has two vowels, the second being final *e,* the first usually has its long sound and the final *e* is not sounded.
- *Ay* at the end of a word has the long sound of /ā/ (may, pay, play).
- When the only vowel in a word (or accented syllable) comes at the end of the word (or syllable), it usually has its long sound.
- When *y* concludes a word of two or more syllables, it has the long sound of /ē/ heard in *lucky* and *badly.*
- *Y* functions as a vowel when it concludes a word or syllable that has no other vowel:

m*y,* sk*y,* d*y* • ing, h*y* • phen

- or falls in the middle of a syllable that has no other vowel:

s*y*m • bol, s*y*n • o • n*y*m, t*y*p • ist

- A diphthong is two adjacent vowels, each of which contributes to the sound heard (h*ou*se, *oi*l, b*oy*).
- The combination *ow* is sometimes pronounced as /ō/ (snow, show); the context provides the major clue to pronunciation.

Chapter 7

STRUCTURAL ANALYSIS SKILLS

*L*earning to read is a long-term, developmental process, and teaching a total word-analysis skills program is also developmental in nature. Previous chapters have presented data on letter-sound relationships; this chapter continues to deal with letter-sound relationships, but we will also stress other important word analysis skills that fit under the broad heading of structural analysis. To maintain normal growth in reading, children must learn to recognize and react to certain features of written language, including inflectional endings (*-s, -ed, -ing, -ly*), compound words, plural forms, prefixes and suffixes, syllabication, contractions, and accent within words.

As we have noted, when children meet a printed word that they do not instantly recognize, they have several options: sounding out the word, using context clues, or combining these two approaches.

Early in beginning reading, children add another option, that of recognizing a root word embedded among affixes. English orthography utilizes a number of structural changes that occur again and again in thousands of words. In learning to read, one must develop expertise in recognizing prefixes, suffixes, and inflectional endings.

To successfully master the structural variations that occur in English orthography, children must come to the reading task with certain skills and abilities. In essence, they must apply or transfer something they already know about letter-sounds and word forms to new situations. For example, assume that a child can recognize the word *ask* but has not yet met *asks, asked,* or *asking.* His prior experience and his ability to respond to *ask* should help him in decoding the inflected forms.

While the child still has the option of sounding out these new words, he also can use the established response to the word *ask.* If one is reading for meaning, this root clue plus the contextual demands of the passage will unlock the inflected forms that are used constantly in the child's oral language.

Different readers, however, will require a differing number of experiences and varied amounts of instruction to acquire the necessary insights. For some children, a prefix and suffix added to a known word tends to obscure what is known. In such cases, more trials are needed for transfer to take place. All children must have a certain amount of practice in recognizing the visual patterns of words that result from the addition of affixes.

One factor that aids both the learner and the teacher is that a great majority of affixes represent the same sound(s) in thousands of different words. Thus, the major objective in working with structural changes in words is to teach children to instantly recognize these visual patterns in written English.

INFLECTIONAL ENDINGS

The word endings -s and -ed represent variations in letter-sound relationships that probably have little impact on learning to read. The fact that final s represents the sound of /s/ in asks and /z/ in dogs is not a cause of confusion to beginners. Nor is the fact that -ed in added, asked, and played is pronounced as ed, t, and d, respectively. The rules that govern these differences are complicated and are much more important to linguists than to native speakers of English whose objective is to learn to read English. Children have never heard, said, or read, "The man work-ed hard" or "Where are my glove-s?"

Nonetheless, children will likely need some practice in visual recognition of inflected word forms because of the structural differences between these and known root words.

Adding -s, -ed, and -ing to Words

1. In the spaces provided, write the word on the left adding -s, -ed, and -ing.
2. Pronounce each word.

Word	-s	-ed	-ing
walk	_____	_____	_____
show	_____	_____	_____
look	_____	_____	_____
ask	_____	_____	_____
call	_____	_____	_____
answer	_____	_____	_____
load	_____	_____	_____
paint	_____	_____	_____

Adding -er, -est, and -ly to Words

1. Make new words by adding the endings -er, -est, and -ly to the root word on the left.
2. Pronounce each word.
3. How do these endings change the meaning of words?

Word	-er	-est	-ly
slow	_____	_____	_____
light	_____	_____	_____
warm	_____	_____	_____
soft	_____	_____	_____
bright	_____	_____	_____
calm	_____	_____	_____

Words ending with e. Drop the final *e* before adding a suffix beginning with a vowel.

Word	+ed	+ing	+er	+est	+ous
bake	baked	baking	baker		
trade	traded	trading	trader		
pale	paled		paler	palest	
fame	famed				famous
late			later	latest	

Adding Suffixes Following *y*

Change *y* to *i* before adding a suffix beginning with a vowel.

Word	Common Endings Beginning with a Vowel			
	-ed	-er	-est	-ous
busy	busied	busier	busiest	
fury				furious
dry	dried	drier	driest	
muddy	muddied	muddier	muddiest	
happy		happier	happiest	
glory				glorious
carry	carried	carrier		

Exception: If the suffix begins with *i*, leave the *y: crying, drying, frying, flying, copying,* and *carrying.*

DOUBLING FINAL CONSONANTS

Explain to children the generalization, "Words that contain one vowel and end with a single consonant (beg, stop, fan) usually double that consonant before adding an ending beginning with a vowel," as in *begged, begging, beggar, stopped, stopping,* and *stopper.*

Teacher: "Look carefully at the words on lines 1, 2, and 3. Add the same endings to the other words."

Word	-ed	-ing	-er
1. log	logged	logging	logger
2. dim	dimmed	dimming	dimmer
3. stop	stopped	stopping	stopper
4. pop	_____	_____	_____
5. skip	_____	_____	_____
6. trot	_____	_____	_____
7. bat	_____	_____	_____
8. trap	_____	_____	_____
9. plan	_____	_____	_____
10. spot	_____	_____	_____

USING CONTEXT

Teacher: "Each of the following sentences has a blank space. Complete each sentence using one word in the clue box that will make the sentence correct."

> **Clue Box**
>
> walks   walked   walk   walking

1. Can the baby _____?

2. Yes, the baby is _____ now.

3. She _____ yesterday.

4. She _____ every day.

5. She will _____ tomorrow.

> **Clue Box**
>
> slow   slowly   slows   slower   slowest

1. Who is the _____ runner on the team?

2. John is very _____ .

3. He is _____ than Tom and Rob.

4. After he runs a while he _____ down.

5. But John is _____ improving.

Teacher: "In the following sentences, write the form of the word that makes the sentence correct."

fast   **1.** John is _____ than Bill, but Ted is the _____ runner on the team.

kind   **2.** The mayor is a _____ old gentleman.

cold   **3.** November is _____ than July.

short   **4.** If they took the _____ trail they should arrive _____ .

long   **5.** What is the _____ word in the dictionary?

Teacher: "Each of these sentences is followed by three words. Two of these words will fit in the blank spaces. Read each sentence and fill in the blanks."

Example:

June is _____ but July is _____ .   warm

June is _____warm_____ but July is _____warmer_____ .   warmer

                                                                            warmest

1. John _____ , "Did anyone _____ for me?"   ask

                                                                            asking

                                                                            asked

2. She _____ yesterday and is also _____ today.   paints

                                                                            painted

                                                                            painting

3. Speaking _____ , John said, "Cotton is _____ than linen."   softer

                                                                            softly

                                                                            softest

4. The car _____ at the _____ sign.   stop

                                                                            stopping

                                                                            stopped

5. It _____ yesterday and is _____ now.   rain

                                                                            rained

                                                                            raining

Teacher: "In each sentence there is a blank space with a root word below it. Add the proper ending to this word so that it will be correct in the sentence."

Example:

Mother is <u>bringing cookies</u>.

1. The bird _____ its wings.
          (flap)

2. We are _____ to leave tomorrow.
                   (plan)

3. We saw a _____ in the woods.
                 (hunt)

4. A man who cuts down trees in a forest is called a _____ .
                                                          (log)

5. One who traps animals is called a _____ .
                                          (trap)

6. The little dog was _____ .
                          (bark)

7. Who is the best _____ on the baseball team?
                       (hit)

8. John is the _____ _____ on the team.
                    (fast)   (run)

9. Two boys were _____ in the sand.
                     (dig)

10. The _____ it rained the _____ we got.
             (hard)   (wet)

COMPOUND WORDS

Mastery of compound words is a developmental process. Children meet a few compounds in first grade and an increasing number thereafter. They need to know that some words are formed by combining two or more words. In most instances, children will be familiar with one or both words that make up a compound.

Recognition of compound words is achieved through every type of word-analysis skill: structural analysis, phonic analysis, and context examination. When teaching compound words, each of these aids should be employed. Learning sight words and structural phonic analysis actually go hand in hand. Keep these points in mind:

- Compound words are part of children's speaking and meaning vocabulary. When they meet compounds in reading, they will combine recognition and sounding techniques.
- The meaning of many compound words is derived from combining two words.
- The pronunciation of the compound word remains the same as for the two combining forms, except for accent or stress.
- Procedures for teaching compound words vary with the instructional level.

BUILDING COMPOUND WORDS

1. Oral Exercise

Purpose: To provide practice in using compound words.

Directions: Explain to children the concept of compound words: combining two or more words to make a different word.

Demonstrate on the chalkboard: some + thing = something
some + one = someone
some + time = sometime

Other words to use include *schoolhouse, barnyard, football, birdhouse, firefighter.*

Teacher: "I'll say a word and you add a word to it to make another word."

1. base _____ (ball)

2. sail _____ (boat)

3. door _____ (way, man, mat)

4. motor _____ (cycle, boat)

5. road _____ (way, side, block)

6. over _____ (head, board, shoe)

7. moon _____ (light, beam, glow)

8. air _____ (plane, port)

9. bath _____ (tub, house, room)

10. tooth _____ (brush, ache, paste)

2. Seeing Compound Words as Wholes and Breaking Them into Parts

Teacher: "Each of the words on the left is a compound word. Write the two words found in each compound word."

Example:

snowman	_____snow_____	_____man_____
1. waterfall	_____	_____
2. bluebird	_____	_____
3. policeman	_____	_____
4. notebook	_____	_____
5. himself	_____	_____
6. homework	_____	_____
7. anyone	_____	_____
8. seaside	_____	_____
9. turnpike	_____	_____
10. airplane	_____	_____

3. More Compound Words

Teacher: "Combine one word from the clue box with each word below the box to form compound words."

Clue Box			
type	tooth	snap	after
any	grand	bed	light

_____ ache   _____ one

_____ noon   _____ writer

_____ father   _____ shot

_____ house   _____ room

To provide practice in recognizing and writing compound words, illustrate how the same word can be used in a number of compound words.

Teacher: "Using the word in the first column, write three compound words."

Example:

air	plane	craft	port
	airplane	*aircraft*	*airport*
1. book	case	keeper	worm
	_____	_____	_____
2. door	way	man	mat
	_____	_____	_____
3. candle	light	maker	stick
	_____	_____	_____
4. moon	glow	beam	light
	_____	_____	_____
5. down	town	wind	stream
	_____	_____	_____
6. shoe	lace	horn	maker
	_____	_____	_____

Teacher: "Each line contains one compound word. Underline the compound word and write it on the blank space at the end of the line."

1. children   dancing   hotdog   _____

2. someone   beaches   crawling   _____

    3. alike   mousetrap   puzzle   _____

    4. downpour   happily   permitted   _____

    5. autumn   mistake   handbag   _____

4. Identifying Compound Words

Directions: Some of the following are compound words, and some are two words written together that do not make a word. Have the children underline the compound words.

beehive	ballback	ballpark
anyelse	everyone	everysome
roommate	roompost	signpost
aftermuch	afternoon	afterman
fireplace	photodog	overland
overleft	houseboat	housemake
nearby	overstill	lifeboat

5. Using Context

Directions: Have the children underline each compound word. Then have them draw a line between the two words in each compound (mail/box).

  1. Everyone went to the football game that afternoon.

  2. Josh is upstairs writing in his scrapbook with his ballpoint pen.

  3. We ran halfway to the clubhouse without stopping.

  4. Doug received a flashlight, a raincoat, and a sailboat for his birthday.

  5. He read the newspaper headline, "Big fire at sawmill."

  6. They saw the shipwreck from a hilltop near the lighthouse.

6. Sentence Completion

Directions: Develop a series of sentences in which a common compound will complete the sentence. Have children read the sentence and write the compound word. Material can be presented orally, or by means of the chalkboard, transparencies, or duplicated exercises. The first exercise is made easy by presenting the compound words in scrambled order above the sentences. In the second exercise, the children provide the words.

baseball	mailbox	bedroom
raincoat	football	seashore

  A.

  1. Letters are mailed in a _____ .

  2. The room we sleep in is called a _____ .

  3. A bat is used in the game of _____ .

4. The girls gathered shells at the _____ .

5. A _____ field has goalposts at each end of the field.

6. Mother said, "It's raining; be sure and wear your _____ ."

B.

1. A player can hit a home run in the game of _____ .

2. The teacher wrote on the _____ with a piece of chalk.

3. The airplane landed at the _____ .

4. The front window in a car is called the _____ .

5. The mailman puts mail in our _____ .

7. Combining Words to Make Compounds

Directions: Have children add the correct word in sentences 1 and 2, then combine those two words in sentence 3.

Example:

1. The opposite of work is _____ . (play)

1

2. In the spring we plant seeds in the _____ . (ground)

2

3. We go to the _____ at recess. (playground)

1 & 2

1. Let's take our sleds and play in the _____ .

1

2. The pitcher threw the _____ over the plate.

2

3. We like to have _____ fights in the winter.

1 & 2

1. The house we live in is called our _____ .

1

2. The opposite of play is _____ .

2

3. School work we do at home is called _____ .

1 & 2

1. A mailman delivers the _____ .

1

2. He carries the mail in a _____ .

2

3. The mailman carries the mail in a _____ .

1 & 2

Teacher: "Each sentence contains a blank space. Select a word from the clue box that will complete a compound word."

Examples:

```
                    Clue Box
      snap        house        grand
```

1. Mother read the letter from our _____ father.

2. The letter contained a _____ shot.

3. It showed our grandfather in front of a light _____ .

```
                         Clue Box
      way         point         wreck         some
      brush       house         teller        star
```

1. John lost his ball_____ pen.

2. The captain gave details about the ship_____ .

3. The sign read, "Don't block the door_____ ."

4. Some of the golfers ate dinner at the club_____ .

5. Susan found a_____fish on the beach.

6. Grandfather was a great story_____ .

7. _____one will have to help the guide.

8. Clean the paint_____ when you finish painting.

WORKING WITH PLURALS

Forming plurals by adding *s, es,* or *ies* results in structural changes in word forms that can be puzzling to children in their early reading experience. Exercises can help children instantly recognize the plurals of common root words.

Adding *-s* to Form Plurals

1. Illustrate the singular-plural concept at the chalkboard using any words to which the letter *-s* is added to form a plural (book—books, hat—hats, chair—chairs). Teach the concept that *plural* means "more than one."

2. Write the plural of each word on the blank space.

cup	_____	game	_____
rat	_____	bag	_____
fan	_____	kitten	_____
boat	_____	comb	_____
desk	_____	nail	_____
rabbit	_____	table	_____
king	_____	ship	_____
crop	_____	sled	_____

3. Prepare materials similar to the illustrations.
4. Read the sentences with the children.

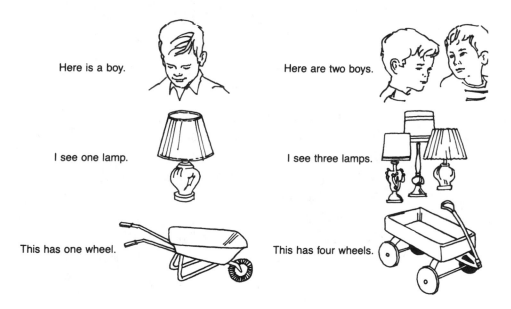

Here is a boy.   Here are two boys.

I see one lamp.   I see three lamps.

This has one wheel.   This has four wheels.

Plurals Formed by Adding -es

Teach the concept that words ending with *s, ss, ch, sh,* and *x* form plurals by the addition of *-es.* Use the chalkboard or duplicated handouts to present material similar to the following.

When do we add *-es* to show more than one?
When words end with

ss	*ch*	*sh*	*x*
dress	church	dish	box
dresses	*churches*	*dishes*	*boxes*

Teacher: "Write the plural for each word."

glass	_____	brush	_____
pass	_____	wish	_____
cross	_____	crash	_____
witch	_____	fox	_____
watch	_____	six	_____
inch	_____	tax	_____

Teacher: "Practice reading these words."

matches	sketches	speeches	benches	waxes
splashes	wishes	batches	ashes	fusses
beaches	kisses	gulches	hisses	birches
bosses	dashes	misses	lashes	gashes

Plurals of Words Ending with *y*

When a word ends with *y,* its plural is formed by changing the *y* to *i* and adding *-es.*

city—cit*ies*   lady—lad*ies*   fairy—fair*ies*

Teacher: "Write the plural for each of these words."

baby	_____	party	_____	cherry	_____
puppy	_____	body	_____	buddy	_____
army	_____	fly	_____	berry	_____

RECOGNITION OF PLURALS

Teacher: "Each of the following words means that there is more than one. These plurals were formed by adding *-s, -es,* or (*y =*) *-ies.* Read these words as quickly as possible."

porches	foxes	cubs	lunches	watches	witches
girls	benches	guesses	coaches	inches	taxes
speeches	peaches	dresses	answers	matches	candies
funnies	factories	cookies	berries	pennies	armies
buses	glasses	frogs	boxes	brushes	dishes

Other Plural Forms

Some plurals involve vowel changes within the word: *foot—feet, man—men, goose—geese, mouse—mice, tooth—teeth,* and *woman—women.*

For words ending with *f*, change *f* to *v* and add *es: wolf—wolves, shelf—shelves, calf—calves, loaf—loaves, thief—thieves,* and *leaf—leaves.*

Some singular and plural forms have the same spelling: *deer—deer, sheep—sheep,* and *moose—moose.*

For words ending with *o* following a consonant, add *es: potato—potatoes, echo—echoes, hero—heroes,* and *zero—zeroes.*

USING CONTEXT

Teacher: "The words in column A each mean that there is only one. If the word under *Clue* means that there is more than one, write the plural of the word in column A on the blank space."

Example:

goose	these	geese
A	*Clue*	
lady	one	
church	many	
city	some	
bench	a	
bird	a flock of	
potato	four	
house	this	
wolf	a pack of	
man	that	
sheep	several	

Teacher: "In each blank space, write the plural form of the underlined word in the sentence."

Examples:

The <u>woman</u> had been speaking to the _____ . (women)

There were many new _____ in the dress shop. (dresses)

1. The board was a <u>foot</u> wide and ten _____ long.
2. Put this <u>dish</u> in with the clean _____ .
3. Many _____ claim to be the "most beautiful <u>city</u>."
4. The young <u>wolf</u> watched the older _____ hunt.
5. This <u>watch</u> is more expensive than the other _____ .
6. The <u>spy</u> story was written by two _____ .

7. There were many _____ in the <u>bus</u> station.

8. He asked the <u>boy</u> where the other _____ were playing.

9. That <u>lady</u> is president of the _____ group.

10. Put all of the smaller _____ in the largest <u>box.</u>

Teacher: "In each blank space, write the plural of the italicized word."

1. There was one *pony* in the pasture.

There were two _____ in the pasture.

2. The police captured a *spy.*

The police captured three _____ .

3. Each *lady* bought a hat.

All the _____ bought hats.

4. One *fly* flew away.

Both _____ flew away.

5. John lost one *penny.*

John lost several _____ .

PREFIXES AND SUFFIXES

As children progress in reading, they will meet many words that contain prefixes and suffixes. Teaching aimed at making each child an independent reader will have to deal with structural analysis, phonic analysis, and syllabication. In addition, the teaching of reading will have to focus on the changes in meaning that result when affixes are added to root words.

Many children develop the attitude that they will be unsuccessful in solving longer polysyllabic words, and they give up easily. Thus, their fears are self-fulfilling. One of the objectives of the following exercises is to provide hints that will help readers unlock such words. Children are led to see that English writing contains many prefabricated units (prefixes and suffixes). A number of clues are pointed out, namely that these affixes are spelled the same in thousands of different words and thus have the same visual pattern, have the same pronunciation in different words, consistently appear before or after a root word, and are usually syllables.

The procedures and materials in example A focus on having children see and combine root words with prefixes and suffixes while pronouncing the words formed. Examples B and C stress syllabication.

A. Each line begins with a root word to which three prefixes are added. The children pronounce these words, noting the visual patterns resulting from the prefixes.

Root	*+ pre*	*+ re*	*+ un*
pack	prepack	repack	unpack
wind	prewind	rewind	unwind
paid	prepaid	repaid	unpaid

Root	+ *dis*	+ *mis*	+ *re*
place	displace	misplace	replace
use	disuse	misuse	reuse
count	discount	miscount	recount

B. The first word in each column is a root word; the second has a common prefix; the third, a common word ending.

Root	+ *dis*	+ *ment*
appoint	dis/appoint	dis/appoint/ment
agree	dis/agree	dis/agree/ment
place	dis/place	dis/place/ment

Root	+ *re*	+ *able*
clean	re/clean	re/clean/able
form	re/form	re/form/able
charge	re/charge	re/charge/able

Root	+ *in*	+ *ness*
complete	in/complete	in/complete/ness
direct	in/direct	in/direct/ness
visible	in/visible	in/visible/ness
human	in/human	in/human/ness

C. The first word in each column is a root word; a suffix has been added in the second; and another suffix in the third.

Root	+ *less*	+ *ness*
use	useless	uselessness
speech	speechless	speechlessness
sight	sightless	sightlessness

Root	+ *ful*	+ *ness*
watch	watchful	watchfulness
truth	truthful	truthfulness
play	playful	playfulness

D. This material stresses the structural (visual) changes resulting from adding affixes. It includes some inflected endings taught previously.
   1. Read each line of words in unison with the class.
   2. Have a volunteer read the same line of words.
   3. Have similar exercises available for individual practice.

agree	agrees	disagree	disagreement	agreeable
fill	refill	filled	refilled	refilling
place	placed	replaced	replacement	places
honor	honorable	dishonor	dishonorable	honored
hope	hopeless	hopeful	hopefully	hoping

E. For practice in building new words by writing common endings, form a new word by writing the ending shown above each group of words.

	-ment			*-ness*	
pay _____	agree _____	blind _____	deaf _____
state _____	pave _____	dry _____	clever _____
move _____	treat _____	close _____	kind _____
enjoy _____	punish _____	bold _____	polite _____
base _____	excite _____	calm _____	like _____

-ful	*-less*	*-able*
hope _____	hope _____	wash _____
cheer _____	cheer _____	honor _____
doubt _____	doubt _____	comfort _____
grace _____	cloud _____	agree _____
dread _____	sleep _____	change _____

USING CONTEXT

Teacher: "Note the underlined word in each clue. Add a prefix and suffix to that word so that the new word fits the clue."

Example:

to not deserve <u>trust</u>.   (un)trust(worthy)

Helpers: | dis   -un- | | -ful   -able   -ment   -ness |

1. you can't avoid it   _____avoid_____
2. a failure to agree   _____agree_____
3. can't depend on him   _____depend_____
4. not being happy is?   _____happi_____
5. does not tell the truth   _____truth_____
6. opposite of or lack of honor   _____honor_____

Teacher: "Note the underlined word in each clue. Add an ending to that word so that the new word fits the clue."

Example:

Some <u>doubt</u> that it will happen.   doubt(<u>ful</u>)

Helpers: | -able   -ful   -less   -ness   -or |

1. no <u>change</u> over the years   change_____

2. can <u>depend</u> on him   depend_____

3. always being <u>idle</u>   idle_____

4. has little or no <u>use</u>   use_____

5. results in <u>pain</u>   pain_____

6. shows <u>grace</u> in dancing   grace_____

To help children achieve mastery of root words plus affixes, use the following paragraphs for reading practice. Read one paragraph, then select a volunteer to read. Tell students, "As we read each paragraph, note the meaning of the underlined words."

The Governor said, "I <u>doubt</u> that the bridge will be built. <u>Doubtless</u>, many of you would like to see it built. However, it is quite <u>doubtful</u> that funds will be available. Informed observers agree that this is <u>doubtlessly</u> true."

<u>Advertisers</u> spend money on <u>advertising</u> because <u>advertisements</u> help to <u>advertise</u> what they have to sell.

A towel will <u>absorb</u> water. This towel is <u>absorbing</u> water. Now it has <u>absorbed</u> about all it can. It <u>absorbs</u> because it is made of <u>absorbent</u> material.

A mountain climber must <u>care</u> about safety. Mountain climbers who <u>care</u> will be <u>careful</u>, not <u>careless</u>. <u>Carelessness</u> in the face of danger does not lead to a <u>carefree</u> climb. When plans are thought out <u>carefully</u>, one is not likely to act <u>carelessly</u>.

For writing practice, tell students to write a paragraph using all (or as many as possible) of the words on each line.

beauty, beautiful, beautifully

joy, joyful, joyfully, joyous, joyless, joylessly

help, helpful, helpfulness, helpless, helplessness

war, prewar, postwar, prowar, antiwar, warlike

SYLLABICATION

A syllable is a vowel or a group of letters containing a vowel sound that together form a pronounceable unit. The ability to break words into syllables is an important word analysis skill that cuts across both phonic and structural analysis. Syllabication is an aid in pronouncing words not instantly recognized as sight words, arriving at the correct spelling of many words, and breaking words at the end of a line of writing.

Two major clues to syllabication are prefixes and suffixes, and certain vowel-consonant behavior in written words. Thus, the ability to solve the pronunciations represented by many longer printed words is built on the recognition of both structural and phonetic features.

Much of the material regarding prefixes and suffixes can be used for teaching syllabication, as well as visual recognition of word parts. This chapter section continues to build recognition of prefixes and suffixes but also stresses how these function as syllables. With practice, syllabication tends to become an automatic process. To illustrate, there will be considerable agreement among adult readers when they pronounce the following nonsense words: *dismorative, unmurly, interlate,* and *motoption.* The syllabication patterns arrived at would probably be *dis·mor·a·tive, un·mur·ly, in·ter·late,* and *mo·top·tion.* In addition, there would probably be relatively high agreement as to which syllable was to receive the primary accent: *dis·mor'·a·tive, un·mur'·ly, in'·ter·late,* and *mo·top'·tion.*

The reader's pronunciation of these nonsense words probably did not involve calling to mind rules that might apply, yet the responses were undoubtedly conditioned by previous learning and experiences that relate to principles of syllabication. Despite numerous exceptions to some generalizations dealing with syllabication, other generalizations may be useful to students aspiring to become independent readers.

Generalizations Relating to Syllabication

1. There are as many syllables in a word as there are vowel sounds. Syllables are determined by the vowel sounds heard, not by the number of vowels seen.

	Vowels Seen		Vowels Heard		Vowels Seen		Vowels Heard
measure	(4)	mezh'er	(2)	moment	(2)	mō' ment	(2)
phonics	(2)	fon iks	(2)	cheese	(3)	chēz	(1)
write	(2)	rīt	(1)	which	(1)	hwich	(1)
release	(4)	rē lēs	(2)	precaution	(5)	prē kô shun	(3)
skill	(1)	skill	(1)	receive	(4)	rē sēv'	(2)

2. Syllables divide between double consonants or between two consonants.

hap·pen	can·non	sud·den	ves·sel	vol·ley	com·mand
bas·ket	tar·get	cin·der	har·bor	tim·ber	wig·wam
don·key	pic·nic	gar·den	lad·der	let·ter	sup·per

3. A single consonant between vowels usually goes with the second vowel.

fa mous	ho tel	di rect	ti ger	ce ment	pu pil
ea ger	wa ter	po lice	lo cate	va cant	spi der
be gin	fi nal	be fore	pi lot	li bel	sto ry
pa rade	e lect	re ceive	lo cal	sta tion	be hind

   The previous two generalizations are often combined: Divide between two consonants and in front of one.

4. As a general rule, do not divide consonant digraphs (*ch, th,* etc.) and consonant blends.

tea*ch* er	wea*th* er	ma *ch*ine	se *cr*et	a *gree*
bro*th* er	prea*ch* er	a*th* lete	coun *try*	cel e *brate*

5. The word endings *-ble, -cle, -dle, -gle, -kle, -ple, -tle,* and *-zle* form the final syllable.

mar ble	mus cle	han dle	sin gle	an kle	tem ple
ket tle	puz zle	no ble	pur ple	bat tle	bu gle

The following list of words can be used in building board or seatwork exercises. Instruct your students to practice these words so they can recognize and pronounce each one instantly. Point out how easy it is to learn to spell the words.

no ble	rat tle	sin gle	han dle	tem ple	an kle
mar ble	ket tle	wig gle	mid dle	ma ple	spar kle
sta ble	ti tle	jun gle	pad dle	ap ple	wrin kle
tum ble	bat tle	strug gle	bun dle	sam ple	sprin kle
trou ble	bot tle	gig gle	fid dle	pur ple	crin kle
fa ble	gen tle	bu gle	bri dle	stee ple	tin kle
dou ble	cat tle	ea gle	nee dle	sim ple	puz zle
rum ble	man tle	an gle	sad dle	un cle	fiz zle
peb ble	set tle	shin gle	kin dle	cir cle	muz zle
bub ble	lit tle	strag gle	pud dle	ve hi cle	daz zle

6. Usually, prefixes and suffixes form separate syllables.

re load ing	un fair	dis agree ment	pre heat ed
hope less	trans port ing	un like ly	ex cite ment

Affixes as Syllables

As we have noted, many prefixes and word endings constitute syllables that are highly consistent in regard to spelling and pronunciation. When children encounter difficulty in attacking and solving longer words, experiences should be provided that help them see the spelling and syllable patterns. The following lessons can help children recognize polysyllabic words that contain a prefix, suffix, or both.

SEEING SYLLABLES IN LONGER WORDS

A. Read down each column.

lo	con	dis
lo co	con ver	dis a
lo co mo	con ver sa	dis a gree
lo co mo tive	con ver sa tion	dis a gree ment

B. Read down each column.

lo	con	dis
lo co	con ver	dis a
lo co mo	con ver sa	dis a gree
lo co mo tive	con ver sa tion	dis a gree ment
lo co mo	con ver sa	dis a gree
lo co	con ver	dis a
lo	con	dis
locomotive	*conversation*	*disagreement*

C. Read across each line as quickly as you can.

locomotive	lo	lo co	lo co mo	locomotive
conversation	con	con ver	con ver sa	conversation
disagreement	dis	dis a	dis a gree	disagreement

D. Note the italicized parts of the first word in each column. The words in each column begin and end with the same prefix and suffix, which in every case are pronounced exactly the same. Reading down the columns, pronounce these words as quickly as you can. This practice will help you recognize and sound out words when you meet them in your reading.

*con*duc*tion*	*re*fill*able*	*dis*appoint*ment*
conformation	remarkable	disagreement
condensation	reclaimable	disarmament
conservation	recoverable	disarrangement
concentration	redeemable	displacement
conscription	recallable	disfigurement
contraction	respectable	discouragement

contribution	reliable	disenchantment
conviction	renewable	disengagement
consolidation	restrainable	discontentment

E. The following words contain prefixes and suffixes, but the words are in mixed order. Also, some prefixes and suffixes may be new to you. Practice pronouncing the words as quickly as you can.

dishonorable	resentment	discernment	remorseless
relentless	preoccupation	resistant	readjustment
premeditate	consolidation	distractible	configuration
reconstruction	distributive	preparatory	reelection
protective	recollection	consignment	disqualification
confederation	presumably	prohibitive	constructive
unseasonable	imperfection	automotive	protectorate
implication	discoloration	concealment	unwholesome

F. Each line consists of long words that contain the same prefix and word ending. The prefixes and suffixes are italicized and the words are broken into syllables. Read each line as quickly as you can, blending the syllables into the proper pronunciation of the word.

con ven *tion, con* sti tu *tion, con* ver sa *tion, con* tri bu *tion*

ex am i na *tion, ex* pe di *tion, ex* cep *tion, ex* hi bi *tion*

dis ap point *ment, dis* a gree *ment, dis* arm a *ment, dis* cour age *ment*

re fill a *ble, re* place a *ble, re* new a *ble, re* pay a *ble*

in ex act *ly, in* sane *ly, in* dis tinct *ly, in* stant *ly*

ABBREVIATIONS

Abbreviations represent a special instance of structural (visual) changes that are found in printed material. Children need to understand the following concepts about abbreviations.

1. They are a short form of writing that represents a longer word or phrase.
2. They are frequently followed by a period.
3. They are not pronounced, but the word the abbreviation stands for is pronounced.

We See	*We Say*	*We See*	*We Say*
Mr.	Mister	Pres.	President
Dr.	Doctor	Gov.	Governor
Ave.	Avenue	St.	Street

One approach for helping children learn and deal with abbreviations is to present a series of related terms, such as measures, language terms, state names, days of the week, names of months, titles, and so on.

Columns A and B illustrate series; column C presents mixed terms.

A		B		C	
Sunday	Sun.	inch	in.	abbreviated	abbr.
Monday	Mon.	pound	lb.	abbreviation	abbrev.
Tuesday	Tues.	mile	mi.	building	bldg.
Wednesday	Wed.	quart	qt.	plural	pl.
Thursday	Thurs.	square foot	sq. ft.	Northwest	N.W.
Friday	Fri.	yard	yd.	mountain	mt.
Saturday	Sat.	pint	pt.	Boulevard	Blvd.

Directions: Write a number of abbreviations on the chalkboard. Have volunteers give the words the abbreviations represent.

Examples:

Pres.	President
Dr.	Doctor
Ave.	_____
sq. yd.	_____
Gov.	_____
etc.	_____
St.	_____
U.S.	_____

Directions: Have the children write the abbreviations for the words listed. If they need help, they can choose from the abbreviations in the clue box.

Clue Box

D.C.	Gov.	Atty.	Prof.	Wk.
Dr.	Bldg.	Ave.	Chap.	Mr.

Mister	_____	Doctor	_____
Building	_____	Governor	_____
Professor	_____	Week	_____
District of Columbia	_____	Avenue	_____
Chapter	_____	Attorney	_____

Teacher: "In the blank space under each underlined word, write the abbreviation of that word."

1. Last <u>Monday</u> the <u>President</u> spoke to the <u>Governor</u>.

   _____   _____   _____

2. To write the <u>plural</u> of <u>pound</u> add an *s*.

   _____   _____

3. The <u>doctor</u> has an office on Elm <u>Avenue</u>.

   _____   _____

4. The words <u>mile</u>, <u>foot</u>, and <u>quart</u> are measures.

   _____   _____   _____

5. The <u>professor</u> lives on <u>Mountain</u> <u>Boulevard</u>.

   _____   _____   _____

RECOGNIZING CONTRACTIONS

In oral language, children both use and understand contractions. In reading, they need to learn the visual patterns involved, along with the following facts about contractions.

- A contraction is a single word that results from combining two or more words.
- A contraction omits one or more letters found in the combining words.
- A contraction contains an apostrophe where a letter or letters have been omitted.
- A contraction carries the same meaning as the long form it represents, but it has its own pronunciation.

Children need practice in seeing and saying the contracted forms so they can eventually master them as sight words. There are three steps in dealing with contractions: (a) seeing words and contractions together, (b) matching words and contractions, and (c) writing contractions.

1. **Seeing Words and Contractions Together**
   Teacher: "Look at the two words in each line of the first column and see how they form a contraction when combined in the second column."

Words	Contractions	Words	Contractions
I am	I'm	do not	don't
you are	you're	does not	doesn't
it is	it's	was not	wasn't
I have	I've	would not	wouldn't
you have	you've	could not	couldn't
they have	they've	should not	shouldn't

2. **Matching Words and Contractions**
Teacher: "Draw a line from the two words in each row of column A to their contraction in column B."

A	B		A	B
does not	I've		let us	wouldn't
I have	doesn't		would not	let's
do not	can't		was not	I'd
I am	don't		could not	wasn't
cannot	I'm		I would	couldn't

3. **Writing Contractions**
Teacher: "Write the contraction for each of the following word pairs."

they are	_____		I have	_____
she is	_____		should not	_____
must not	_____		here is	_____
will not	_____		they have	_____

Teacher: "In the blank following each sentence, write the contraction for the italicized words."

Example:

Bill *cannot* go swimming. <u>can't</u>

1. *We will* be careful with our campfire. _____
2. Sue *did not* brush her teeth after breakfast. _____
3. *Let us* have a sack race. _____
4. They *could not* catch a fish. _____
5. *I have* eaten my lunch already. _____
6. Larry *does not* play in the street. _____
7. *I am* very happy to see you. _____
8. Karen and Jeff *were not* ready to sing. _____
9. This *is not* my house. _____
10. They *do not* seem very friendly. _____

FINDING LITTLE WORDS IN BIG WORDS

In the past, considerable confusion has arisen over a particular practice. It was once quite common, in materials prepared for teachers, to suggest that children be taught to look for little words in big words. The theory was that after children had learned to recognize smaller words, it would be useful to them as readers if they would see these smaller units when they were part of larger words. This, it was alleged, would help children solve or pronounce the larger words.

This practice, of course, has only limited utility or justification. It is justifiable when dealing with compound words or known root words to which prefixes or suffixes have been added. In general, however, the habit of seeing little words in big words will actually interfere with sounding out words in a great many cases. This is true even in beginning reading.

To illustrate, let us look at some of the more common "little words." In each of the following, if children see and pronounce the little word, they cannot arrive at the pronunciation of the word under attack.

at:	bo at	b at h	pl at e	o at	at e	at omic
	r at e	pot at o	co at	at hlete	he at	
as:	bo as t	ple as e	As ia	co as t	as hore	
on:	on e	t on e	d on e	h on ey	st on e	
he:	he at	he lp	c he st	bat he	t he y	w he at
me:	me at	a me n	ca me	sa me	a me nd	

Hundreds of other examples could be added, using the previous list of little words and many others, such as *in, an, it, am, if, us, is, to, up, go, no, lid, are,* and *or.* Little words (or their spellings) occur frequently in larger polysyllabic words, but the pronounceable autonomy of the little words in big words is often lost. Therefore, teaching children to look for little words in big words has little justification from the standpoint of phonic or structural analysis.

ACCENT

Every syllable in polysyllabic words is not spoken with the same force or stress. These variations in stress are called *accent.* The syllable that receives the most stress is said to have the primary accent (*car'* pen ter). Other syllables in a word may have a secondary accent, or syllables may be unaccented (in' vi *ta'* tion).

Teaching accent is usually reserved for the later stages of word analysis. The majority of words met in beginning reading consist of one or two syllables; longer words are those a child has probably heard or spoken hundreds of times (*yesterday, grandmother, afternoon, tomorrow, telephone*).

Accent is important in using a dictionary when the objective is to determine a word's pronunciation. It is important in reading when children meet words they do not know on sight, but have heard and whose meanings they know. For instance, if children have heard or used the words *celebration* and *appendicitis* but do not recognize the printed symbols, they may distort the pronunciation through improper syllabication: *cē leb' ra tion* rather than *cel e' bra' tion;* or improper accent: *ap' pen di ci tis.*

Skills to be taught include the following.

1. How to read primary and secondary accent marks in the dictionary.
2. The habit of trying different soundings if the first attempt does not result in a known word.
3. The use of clues or rules of accent in attempting the pronunciation of words.

Such clues and rules include:

- In compound words, the primary accent usually falls on (or within) the first word (sail' boat, wolf' hound, fish' er man, door' way).
- In two-syllable words containing a double consonant, the accent usually falls on the first syllable (cop' per, mil' lion, pret' ty, val' ley, sud' den).
- When *ck* ends a syllable, that syllable is usually accented (chick' en, rock' et, pack' age, nick' el, mack' er el).
- Syllables comprised of a consonant plus *le* are usually not accented (*ble, cle, dle, gle, ple, tle*).
- Many of the instances covered by the preceding rules might be summarized under one inclusive generalization: In two-syllable root words, the accent usually falls on the first syllable, except when the second syllable contains two vowels (pa rade', sur prise', sus tain', ma chine', sup pose').
- Prefixes and suffixes are usually not accented (lone' ly, un hap' pi ly, re fresh' ment, dis re spect' ful, re tract' a ble).
- Two-syllable words ending with *y* are usually accented on the first syllable (cit' y, ear' ly, ba' by, can' dy, sto' ry, par' ty, fun' ny, mer' ry, tru' ly).

Shift in Accent

Adding suffixes to some longer words may cause a shift in the primary accent. The words in the left-hand column have the primary accent on the first or second syllables, but in the right-hand column, the accent has shifted.

u' ni verse	u ni ver' sal
mi' cro scope	mi cro scop' ic
vac' ci nate	vac ci na' tion
ac' ci dent	ac ci den' tal
con firm'	con fir ma' tion

We can thus generalize that in many longer words, the primary accent falls on the syllable before the suffix. Exception: In most cases, the primary accent falls two syllables before the suffix *-ate:* ag' gra vate, dom' i nate, ed' u cate, hes' i tate, med' i tate, and op' er ate.

Homographs and accent shift.   Homographs are words with identical spellings, different meanings, and, in some cases, different pronunciations. Note in the following sentences that usage or context determines the pronunciation. Changes may occur in accent or in both accent and syllabication. For example, present = pre/sent' or pres'/ent; content = con/tent' or con'/tent.

1. The mayor was *present* to *present* the awards.
2. The editor was not *content* with the *content* of the article.

3. Always be careful to *address* the letter to the correct *address*.

The following words can be used in exercises when context is provided.

protest—protest	annex—annex
perfect—perfect	rebel—rebel
convict—convict	object—object
permit—permit	contract—contract
excuse—excuse	produce—produce
subject—subject	conduct—conduct

STRESS ON WORDS WITHIN SENTENCES

When working on the accents of syllables within words, one might point out the parallel of stress on words within sentences. While this is not usually seen as a word analysis skill, it is a most important factor in mastering the reading process. Concomitant teaching of accent and stress may help children understand both concepts. Simple sentences might be placed on the board. Children should read the sentences, place added stress on each underlined word, and note the effect of the stress on the melody of the sentence.

This is very bad news.

This is very bad *news*.

This is *very* bad news.

This is very *bad* news.

USE OF THE DICTIONARY AS A WORD ATTACK SKILL

As children become independent readers, they are likely to meet a number of words that they do not know or use in their speaking vocabularies or they cannot easily solve by applying phonic generalizations.

Because the dictionary is a source for pronunciation of words, certain dictionary skills are, in effect, word analysis skills. Effective use of the dictionary involves learning the speech equivalents of visual symbols, including primary and secondary accent marks and other diacritical marks, such as the macron (̄) (make = māk), the breve (̆) (ăt), and the schwa (ə) (ten dər).

Different dictionaries and glossaries in textbooks may use a variety of symbols, or phonetic spellings, all of which will have to be mastered. For example,

technique: tek nēk, těk nēk, tek neek

temperament: tem′ pər ə mənt, těm pēr ment

(For a discussion of the schwa sound, see Chapter 6).

Children should be taught word attack skills using the same pronunciation key that is found in the dictionaries they use. The dictionary will be of little value in arriving at the correct pronunciation of words if these various symbols are not mastered.

SUMMARY

Teaching the decoding process involves more than just letter-sound relationships. Children must also learn to recognize and respond quickly to a number of frequently occurring visual patterns found in English writing. These include inflectional endings, plurals, contractions, abbreviations, prefixes, and suffixes.

After many experiences with affixes (which are also syllables), successful readers develop the ability to treat these word parts as units rather than decoding the same set of letters separately each time they encounter the letters. Thus, in teaching structural analysis skills, the goal is to provide experiences that lead children to this type of behavior. The structural changes that occur over and over in English writing must be instantly recognized. Fortunately, many of these high-frequency affixes have a high degree of consistency in both their visual patterns and sounds.

Bibliography

Adams, M. J. (1990). *Beginning to read: Thinking and learning about print.* Cambridge, MA: MIT Press.

Bailey, M. H. (1967). The utility of phonic generalizations in grades one through six. *Reading Teacher, 20,* 413–418.

Bloomfield, L., & Barnhart, C. (1961). *Let's read: A linguistic approach.* Detroit, MI: Wayne State University Press.

Bruner, J. S. (1972). Address to the International Reading Association Convention. Detroit.

Burmeister, L. E. (1968). Vowel pairs. *Reading Teacher, 21,* 445–452.

Burrows, A., & Lourie, Z. (1963) When two vowels go walking. *Reading Teacher, 17,* 79–82.

Busink, Ria. (1997) Reading and phonological awareness: What we have learned and how we can use it. *Reading Research and Instruction, 36*(3), 199–215.

Chall, J. S. (1989). Learning to read: The great debate 20 years later. *Phi Delta Kappan, 70,* 521–538.

Clymer, T. (1963). The utility of phonic generalizations in the primary grades. *Reading Teacher, 16,* 252–258.

Cunningham, P. M. (1990). The names test: A quick assessment of decoding ability. *Reading Teacher, 44,* 124–129.

Cunningham, P. M., & Cunningham, J. W. (1992). Making words: Enhancing the inverted spelling-decoding connection. *Reading Teacher, 46,* 106–115.

Downing, J. A. (1963). *Experiments with Pitman's initial teaching alphabet in British schools.* New York: Initial Teaching Alphabet Publications.

Downing, J. A. (May, 1965). Common misconceptions about i.t.a. *Elementary English, 42,* 492–501.

Downing, J. A. (December, 1967). Can i.t.a. be improved? *Elementary English, 44,* 849–855.

Early, M. (1993). What ever happened to . . .? *Reading Teacher, 46,* 302–308.

Emans, R. (1967). The usefulness of phonic generalizations above the primary grades. *Reading Teacher, 20,* 419–425.

Flesch, R. (1955). *Why Johnny can't read.* New York: Harper.

Fries, C. C. (1963). *Linguistics and reading.* New York: Holt, Rinehart, & Winston.

Gattengo, C. (1962). *Words in color.* Chicago: Learning Materials.

Goodman, K. S. (1992). I didn't found whole language. *Reading Teacher, 46,* 188–198.

Heilman, A. W. (1977). *Principles and practices of teaching reading,* 4th ed. Columbus, OH: Merrill.

Hempenstall, Kerry. (1997). The whole language–phonics controversy: A historical perspective. *Educational Psychology, 17,* 399–418.

Manning, J. C. (1995). Ariston metron. *Reading Teacher, 48,* 650–659.

Moustafa, M. (1993). Recoding in whole language reading instruction. *Language Arts, 70,* 483–487.

Newman, J. M., & Church, S. M. (1990). Myths of whole language. *Reading Teacher, 44,* 20–26.

Oaks, R. E. (1952). A study of the vowel situations in a primary vocabulary. *Education, 72,* 604–617.

Pollard, R. (1889). *Pollard's synthetic method.* Chicago: Western Publishing House.

Programmed reading (n.d.). Webster Division, McGraw-Hill.

Reading Teacher. (1991). Beginning to read: A critique by literacy professionals and a response by Marilyn Jager Adams, *44,* 366–395.

Richgels, D. J., Poremba, K. J., & McGee, L. M. (1996). Kindergartners talk about print: Phonemic awareness in meaningful contexts. *Reading Teacher, 49,* 632–642.

Samuels, S. J. (1988). Decoding and automaticity: Helping poor readers become automatic at word recognition. *Reading Teacher, 41,* 756–760.

Smith, F. (1973). *Psycholinguistics and reading.* New York: Holt, Rinehart, & Winston.

Smith, N. B. (1934). *American reading instruction.* New York: Silver Burdett.

Spiegel, D. L. (1992). Blending whole language and systematic direct instruction. *Reading Teacher, 46,* 38–44.

Stahl, S. A. (1992). Saying the "P" word: Nine guidelines for exemplary phonics instruction. *Reading Teacher, 45,* 618–625.

Stahl, S. A., Osborn, J., & Lehr, F. (1990). *Beginning to read: Thinking and learning about print—a summary.* Champaign, IL: University of Illinois.

Stanovich, K. E. (1993). Romance and reality. *Reading Teacher, 47,* 280–291.

Strickland, D. S. (1994). Reinventing our literacy programs: Books, basics, balance. *Reading Teacher, 48,* 294–302.

Troia, Gary A. (1999). Phonological awareness intervention research: A critical review of the experimental methodology. *Reading Research Quarterly, 34,* 28–52.

Veatch, J. (1996). From the vantage of retirement. *Reading Teacher, 49,* 510–516.

Walmsley, S. A. and Adams, E. L. (1993). Realities of whole language. *Language Arts, 70,* 272-280.

Wood, Clare, & Terrell, Colin. (1998). Pre-school phonological awareness and subsequent literacy development. *Educational Psychology, 18,* 253–74.

Yopp, H. K. (1992). Developing phonemic awareness in young children. *Reading Teacher, 45,* 696–703.

Yopp, H. K. (1995). A test for assessing phonemic awareness in young children. *Reading Teacher, 49,* 20–28.

Index